ABT

P9-EEC-589

1008

The Oregon Trail

written by **Joeming Dunn**
illustrated by **Tim Smith III**

visit us at
www.abdopublishing.com

Published by Magic Wagon, a division of the ABDO Publishing Group, 8000 West 78th Street, Edina, Minnesota 55439. Copyright © 2009 by Abdo Consulting Group, Inc. International copyrights reserved in all countries. All rights reserved. No part of this book may be reproduced in any form without written permission from the publisher.
Graphic Planet™ is a trademark and logo of MagicWagon.

Printed in the United States.

Written by Joeming Dunn
Illustrated by Tim Smith III
Edited by Stephanie Hedlund and Rochelle Baltzer
Interior layout and design by Antarctic Press
Cover art by Rod Espinosa
Cover design by Neil Klinepier

Library of Congress Cataloging-in-Publication Data

Dunn, Joeming W.
  The Oregon Trail / written by Joeming Dunn ; illustrated by Tim Smith, III.
     p. cm. -- (Graphic history)
  Includes bibliographical references and index.
  ISBN 978-1-60270-183-0
 1. Oregon National Historic Trail--History--Juvenile literature. 2. Overland journeys to the Pacific--Juvenile literature. 3. Pioneers--Oregon National Historic Trail--History--19th century--Juvenile literature. 4. Pioneers--Oregon National Historic Trail--Social life and customs--19th century--Juvenile literature. 5. Frontier and pioneer life--Oregon National Historic Trail--Juvenile literature. I. Smith, Tim, 1974- II. Title.
F597.D86 2008
978'.02--dc22
                        2007051652

TABLE of CONTENTS

Timeline

1804-1806 - William Clark and Meriwether Lewis explored the lands west of the Missouri River.

1818 - The United States and Great Britain agreed to joint occupation of the Oregon Territory.

1825 - Fort Vancouver was built along the Columbia River.

1834 - Marcus and Narcissa Whitman and Henry and Eliza Spalding set up a mission at the junction of the Columbia and Snake rivers. Their travel route would become known as the Oregon Trail.

1841 - The first emigrant party, the Bidwell-Bartleson party, left for California and Oregon.

1843 - The Great Migration was led by Dr. Marcus Whitman. It was a rush of approximately 1,000 pioneers who headed out on the Oregon Trail.

1848 - Oregon became an official U.S. territory.

1859 - Oregon joined the Union as a state.

1861 - The battle at Fort Sumter marked the beginning of the Civil War.

1869 - The transcontinental railroad was completed. The Oregon Trail was no longer needed.

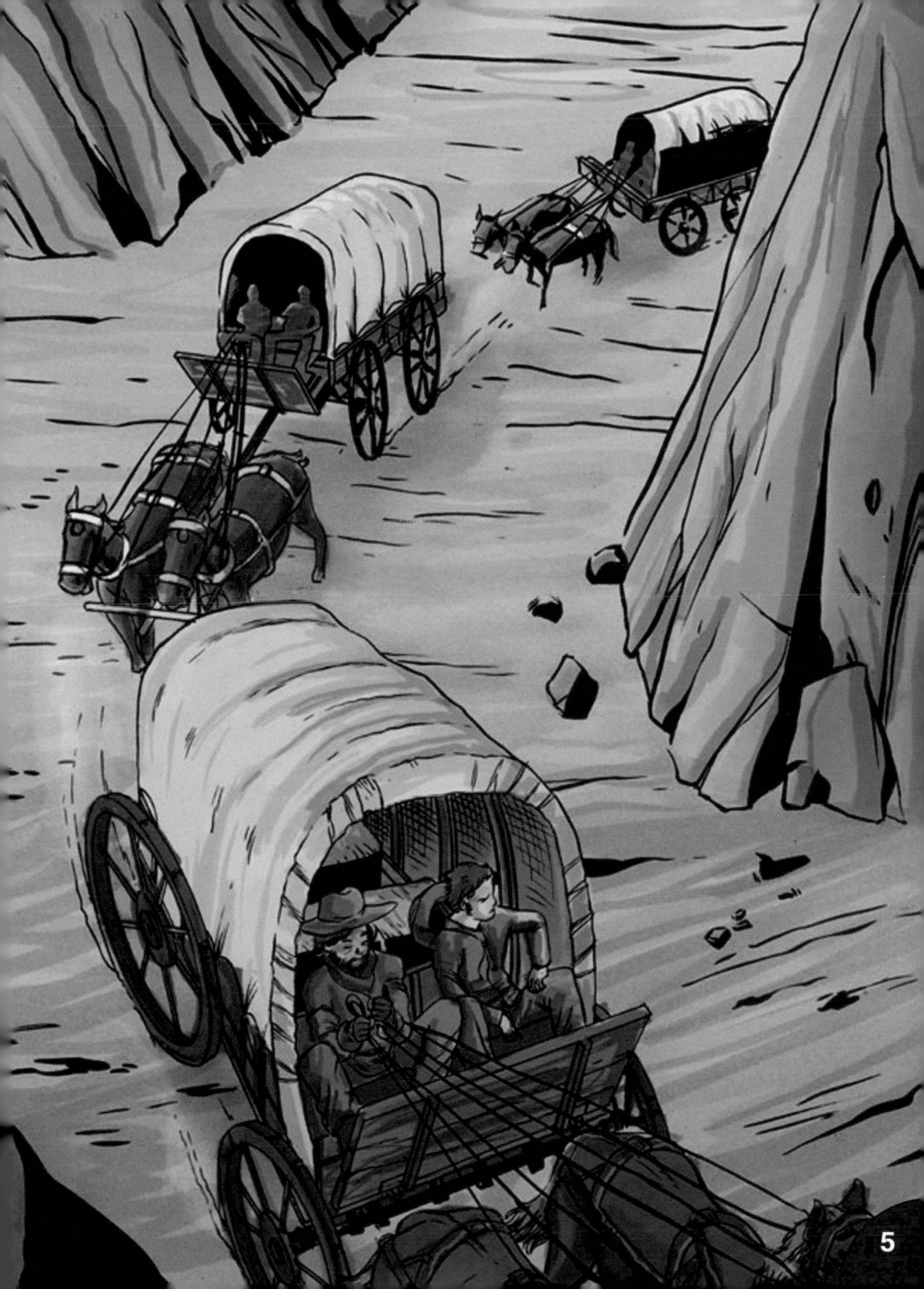

Chapter 1 The Louisiana Purchase

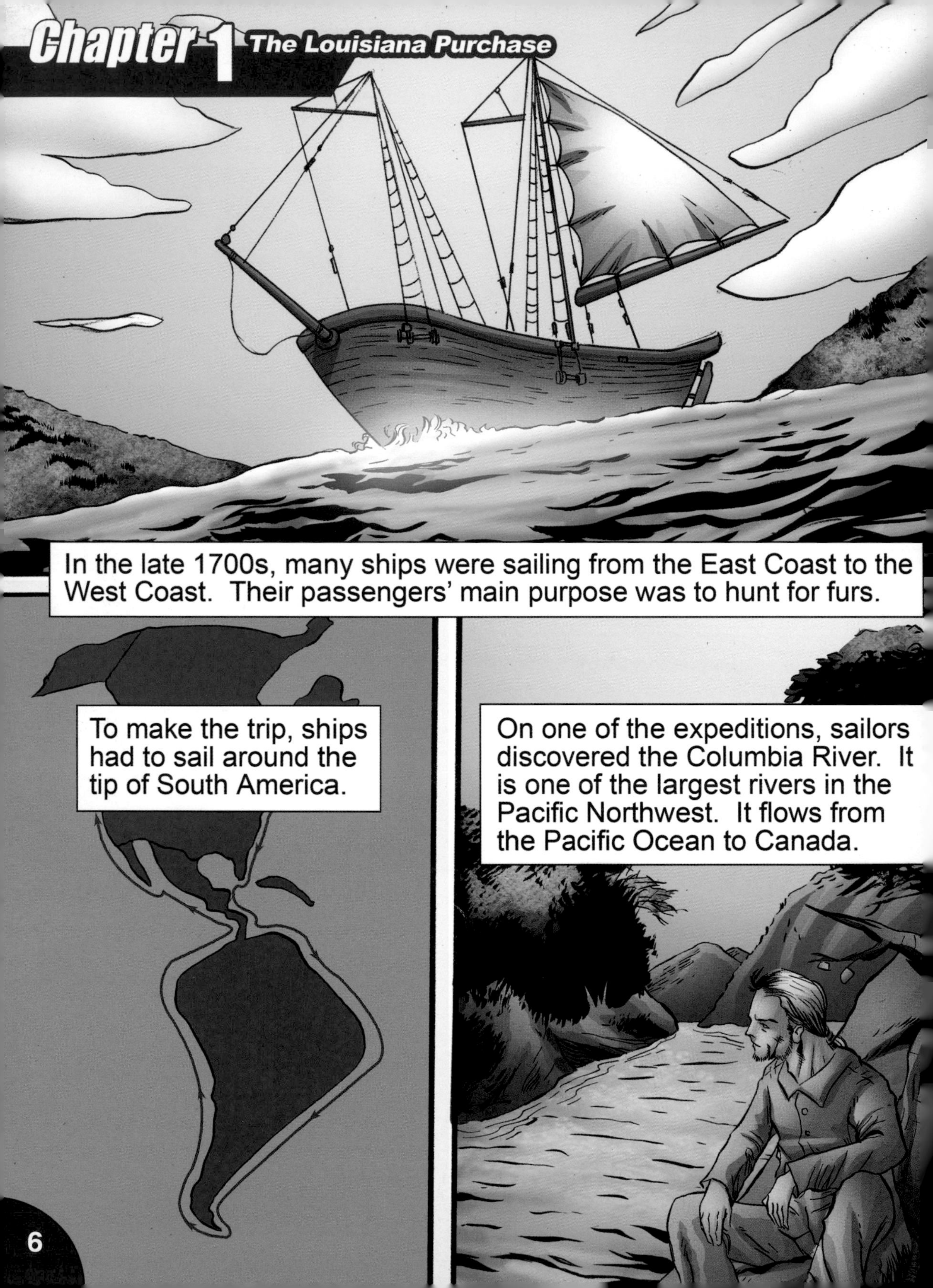
In the late 1700s, many ships were sailing from the East Coast to the West Coast. Their passengers' main purpose was to hunt for furs.
To make the trip, ships had to sail around the tip of South America.
On one of the expeditions, sailors discovered the Columbia River. It is one of the largest rivers in the Pacific Northwest. It flows from the Pacific Ocean to Canada.

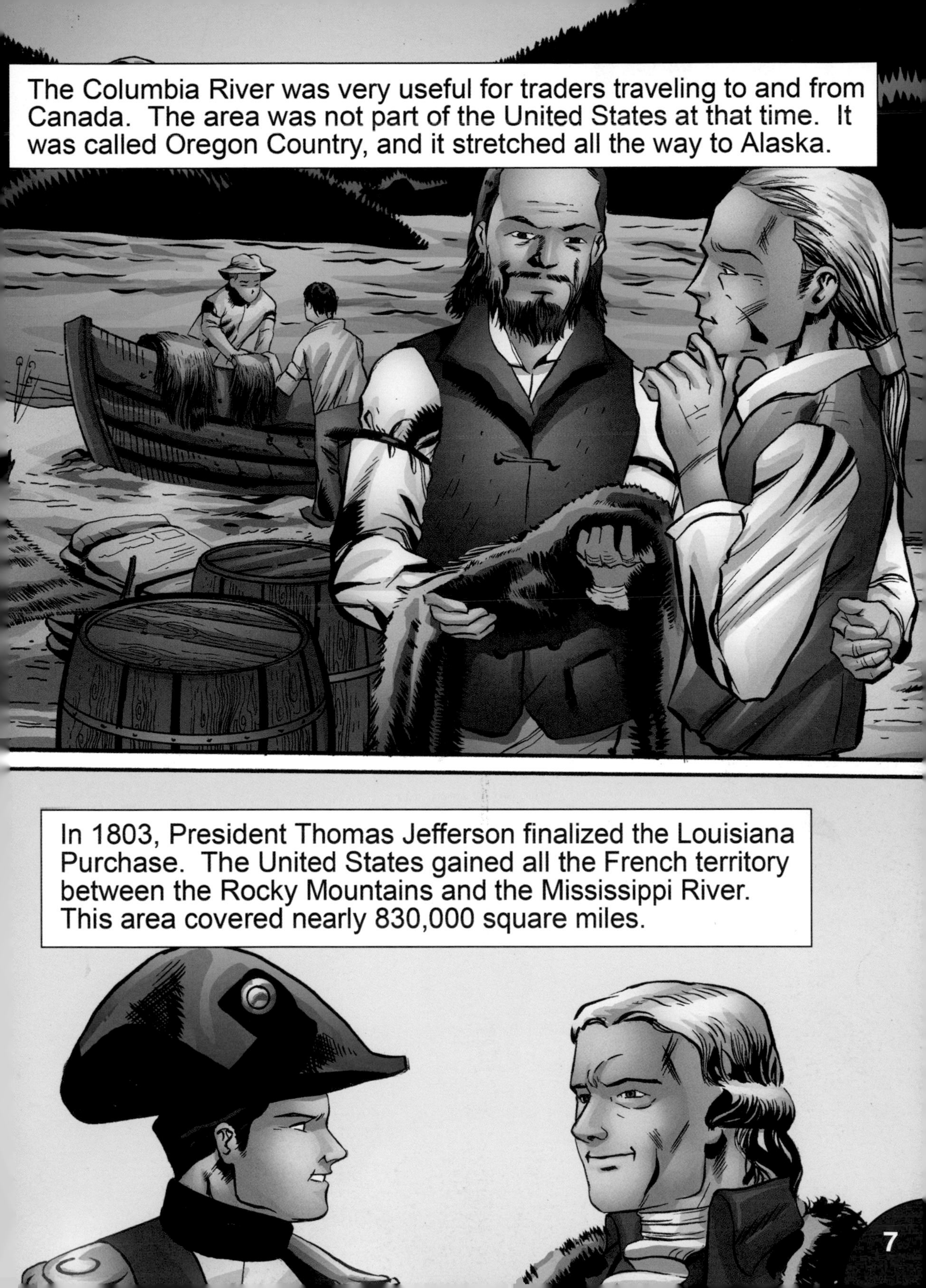
The Columbia River was very useful for traders traveling to and from Canada. The area was not part of the United States at that time. It was called Oregon Country, and it stretched all the way to Alaska.
In 1803, President Thomas Jefferson finalized the Louisiana Purchase. The United States gained all the French territory between the Rocky Mountains and the Mississippi River. This area covered nearly 830,000 square miles.

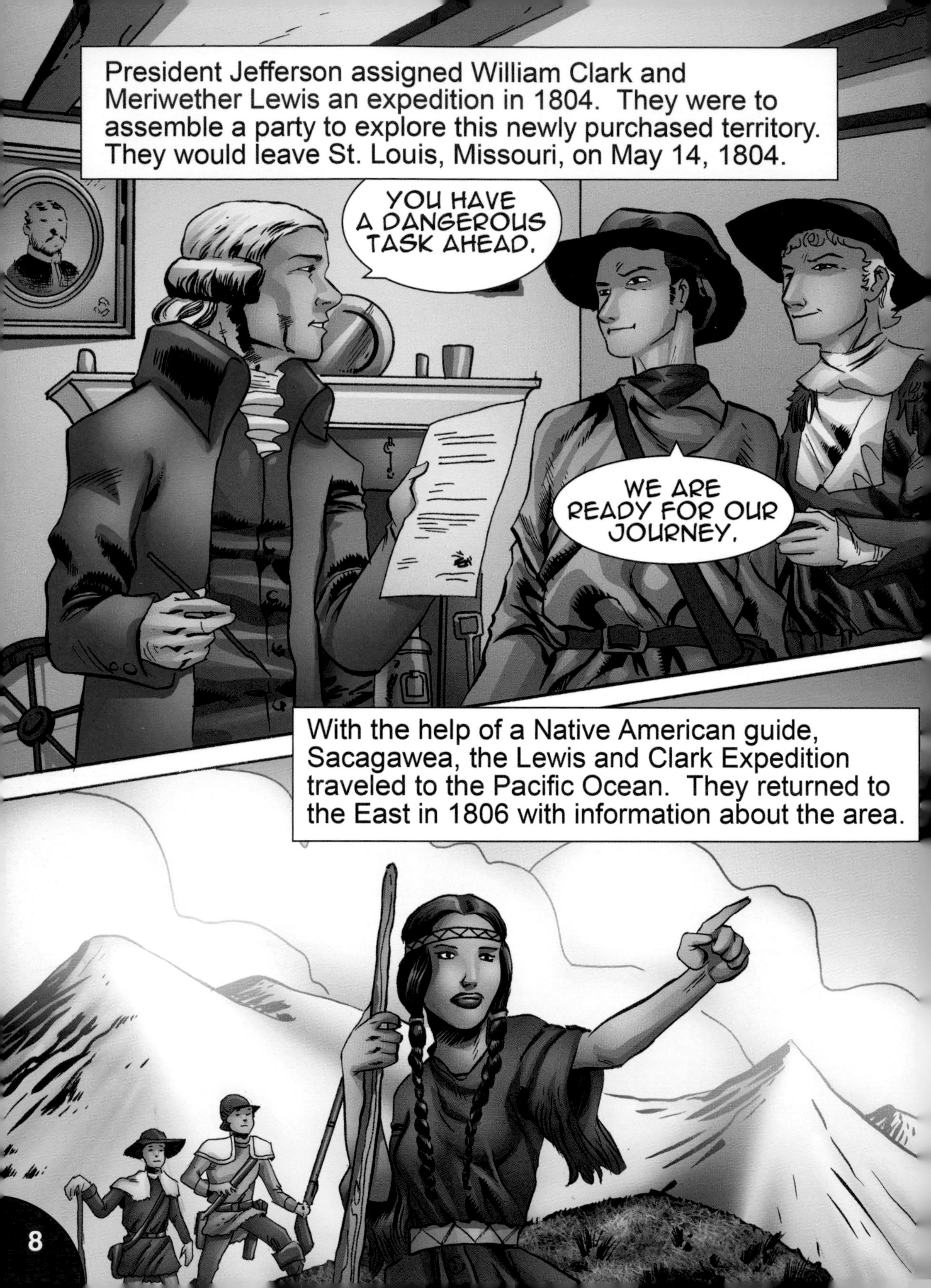
President Jefferson assigned William Clark and Meriwether Lewis an expedition in 1804. They were to assemble a party to explore this newly purchased territory. They would leave St. Louis, Missouri, on May 14, 1804.
YOU HAVE A DANGEROUS TASK AHEAD.
WE ARE READY FOR OUR JOURNEY.
With the help of a Native American guide, Sacagawea, the Lewis and Clark Expedition traveled to the Pacific Ocean. They returned to the East in 1806 with information about the area.

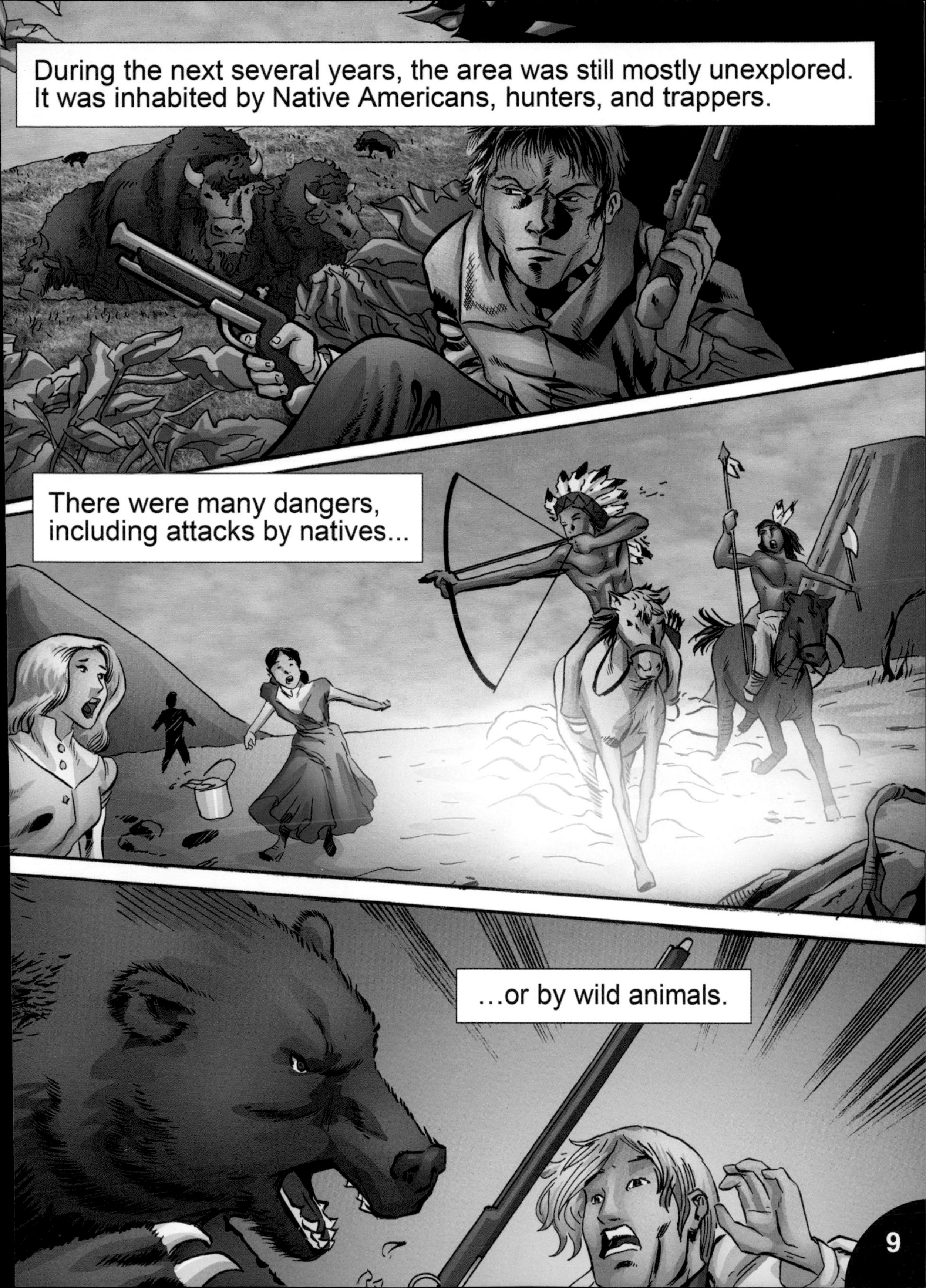
During the next several years, the area was still mostly unexplored. It was inhabited by Native Americans, hunters, and trappers.
There were many dangers, including attacks by natives...
...or by wild animals.

Chapter 2 Transporting Furs

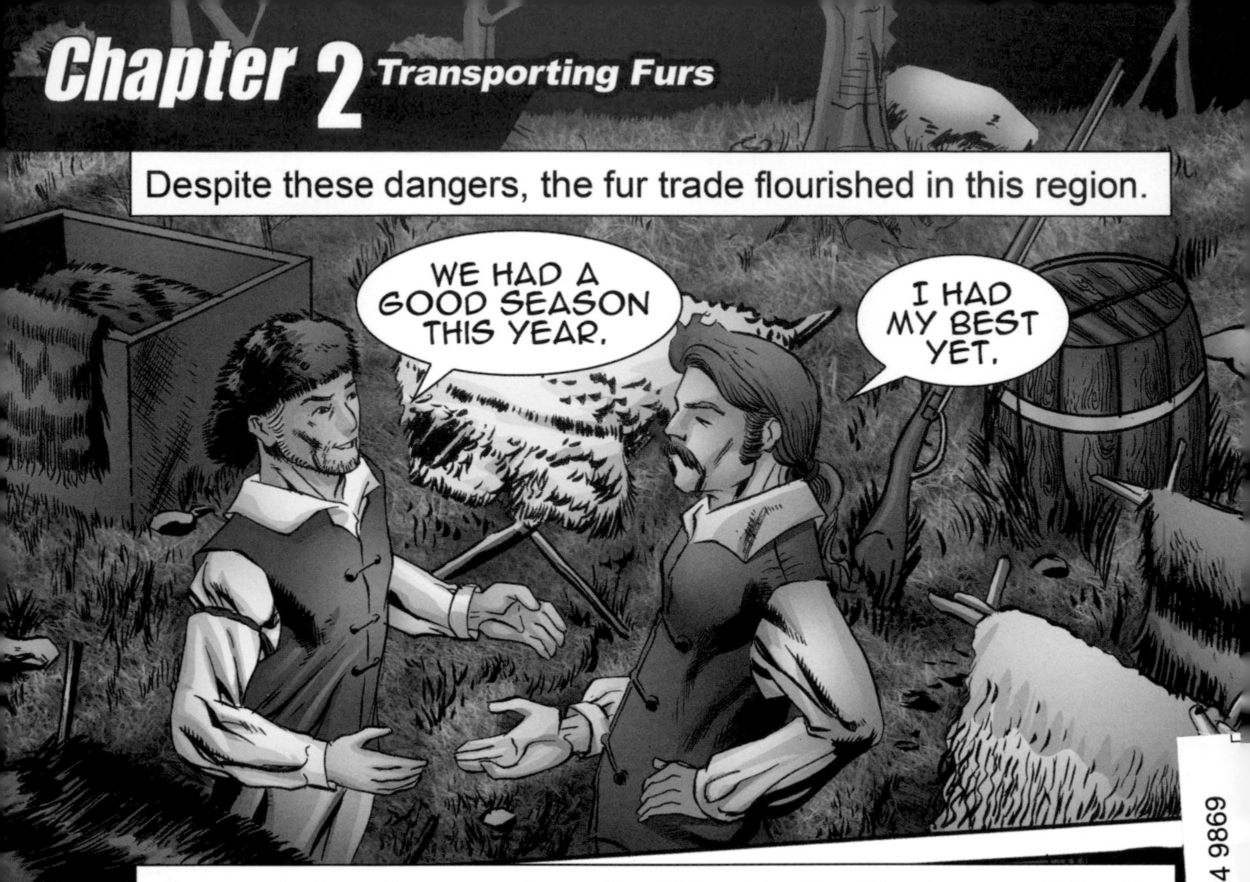
Despite these dangers, the fur trade flourished in this region.
WE HAD A GOOD SEASON THIS YEAR.
I HAD MY BEST YET.

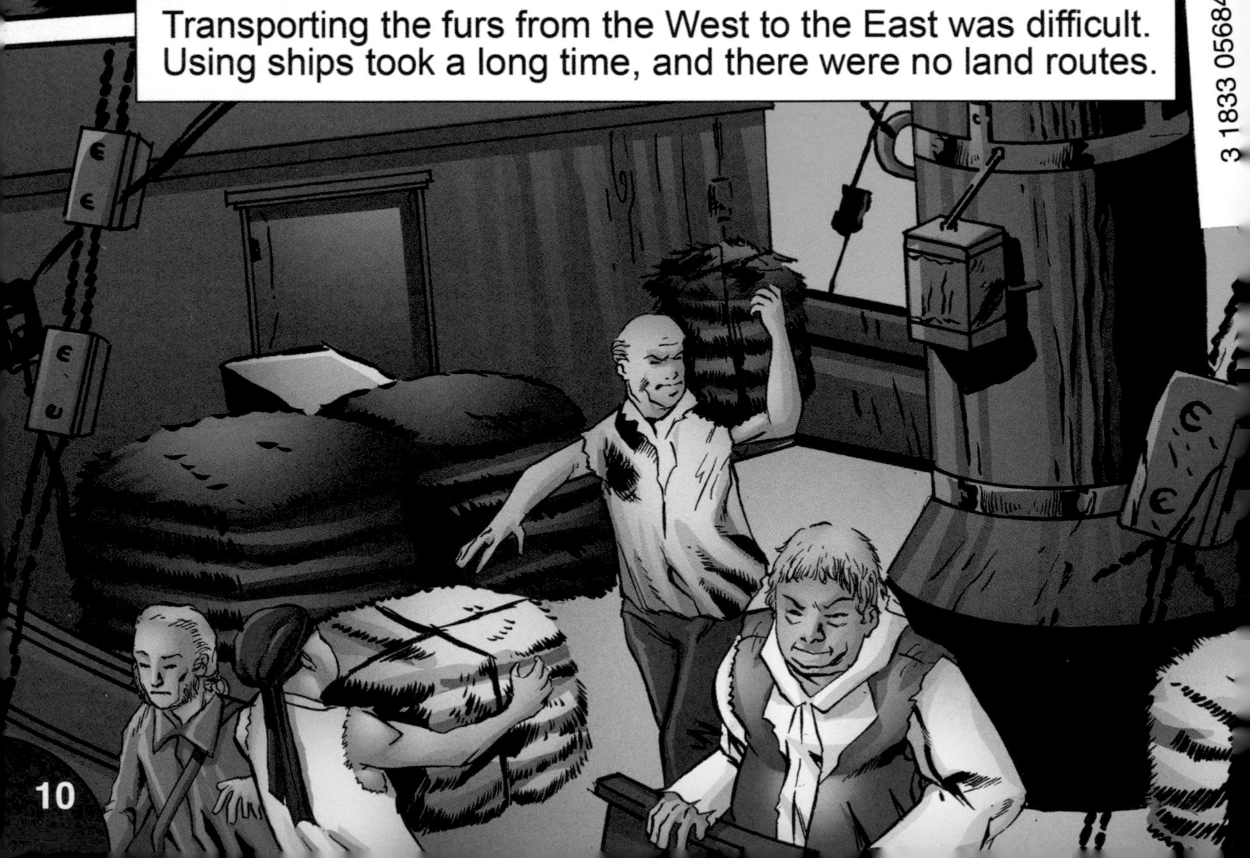
Transporting the furs from the West to the East was difficult. Using ships took a long time, and there were no land routes.

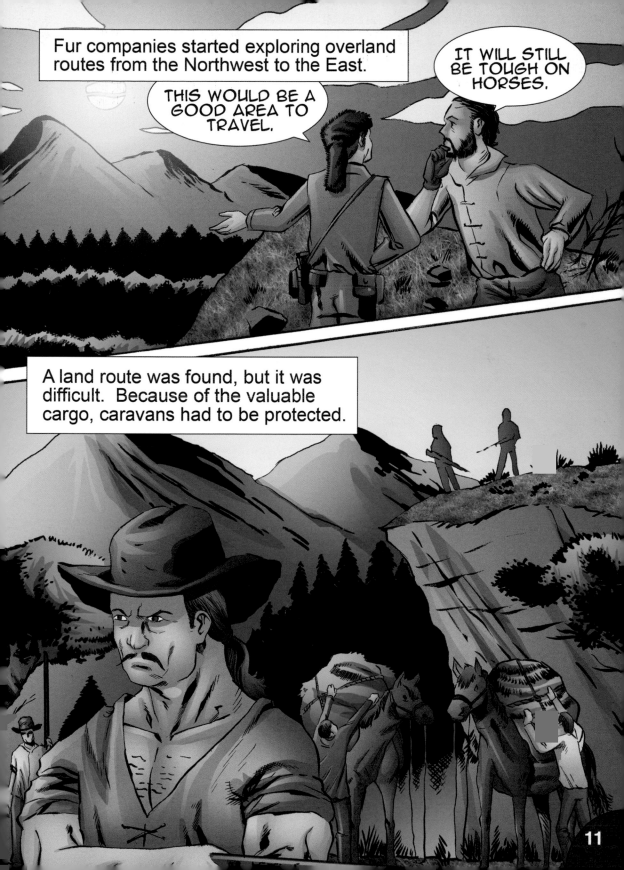

Fur companies started exploring overland routes from the Northwest to the East.

THIS WOULD BE A GOOD AREA TO TRAVEL.

IT WILL STILL BE TOUGH ON HORSES.

A land route was found, but it was difficult. Because of the valuable cargo, caravans had to be protected.

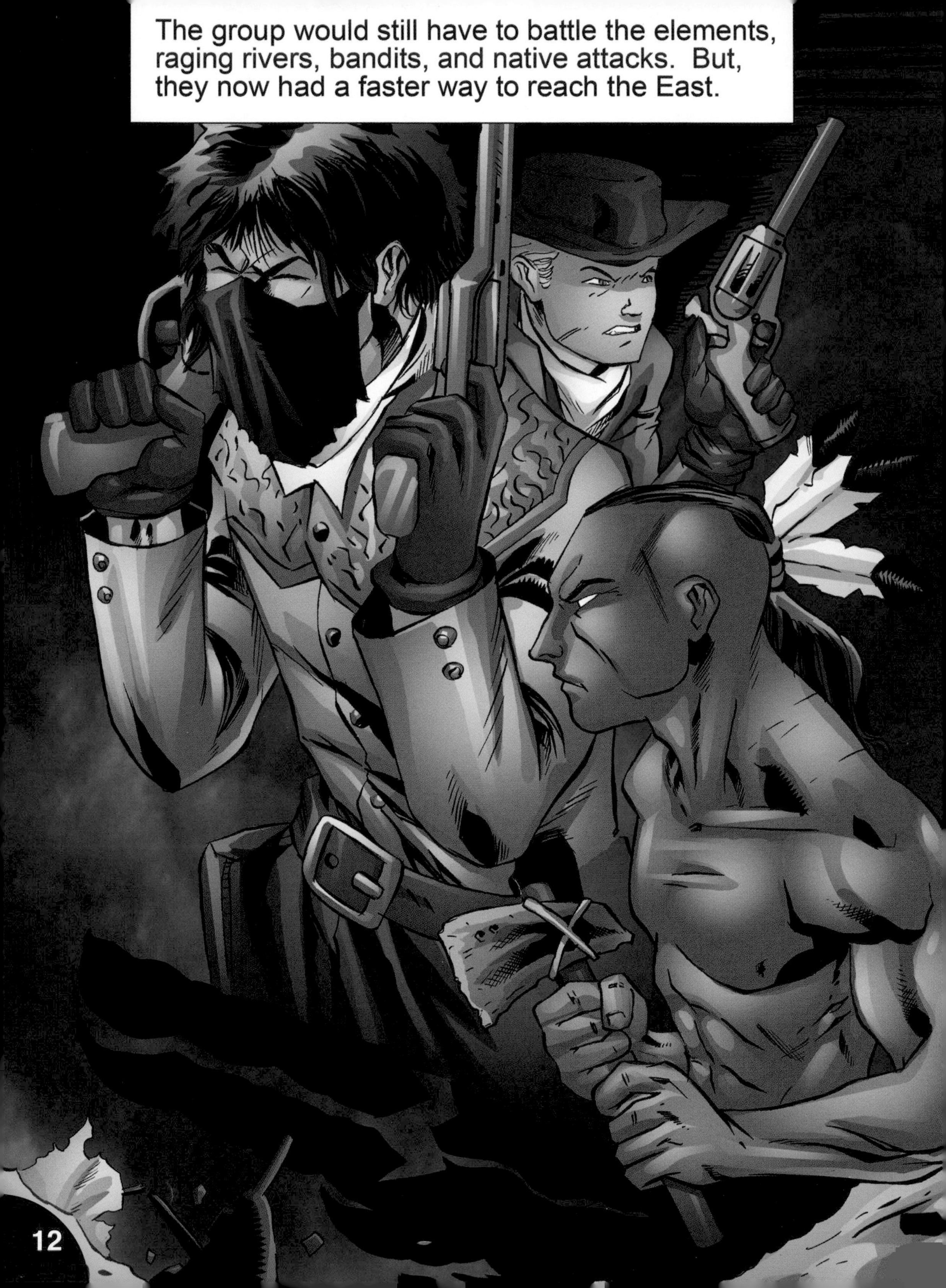
The group would still have to battle the elements, raging rivers, bandits, and native attacks. But, they now had a faster way to reach the East.

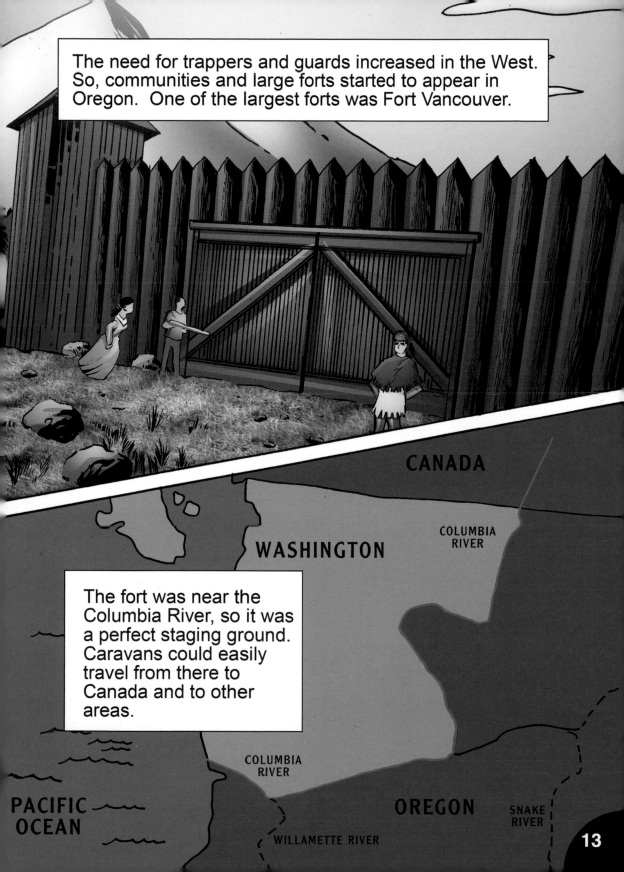

The need for trappers and guards increased in the West. So, communities and large forts started to appear in Oregon. One of the largest forts was Fort Vancouver.

The fort was near the Columbia River, so it was a perfect staging ground. Caravans could easily travel from there to Canada and to other areas.

CANADA

WASHINGTON

COLUMBIA RIVER

COLUMBIA RIVER

PACIFIC OCEAN

OREGON

SNAKE RIVER

WILLAMETTE RIVER

Chapter 3 Missionaries

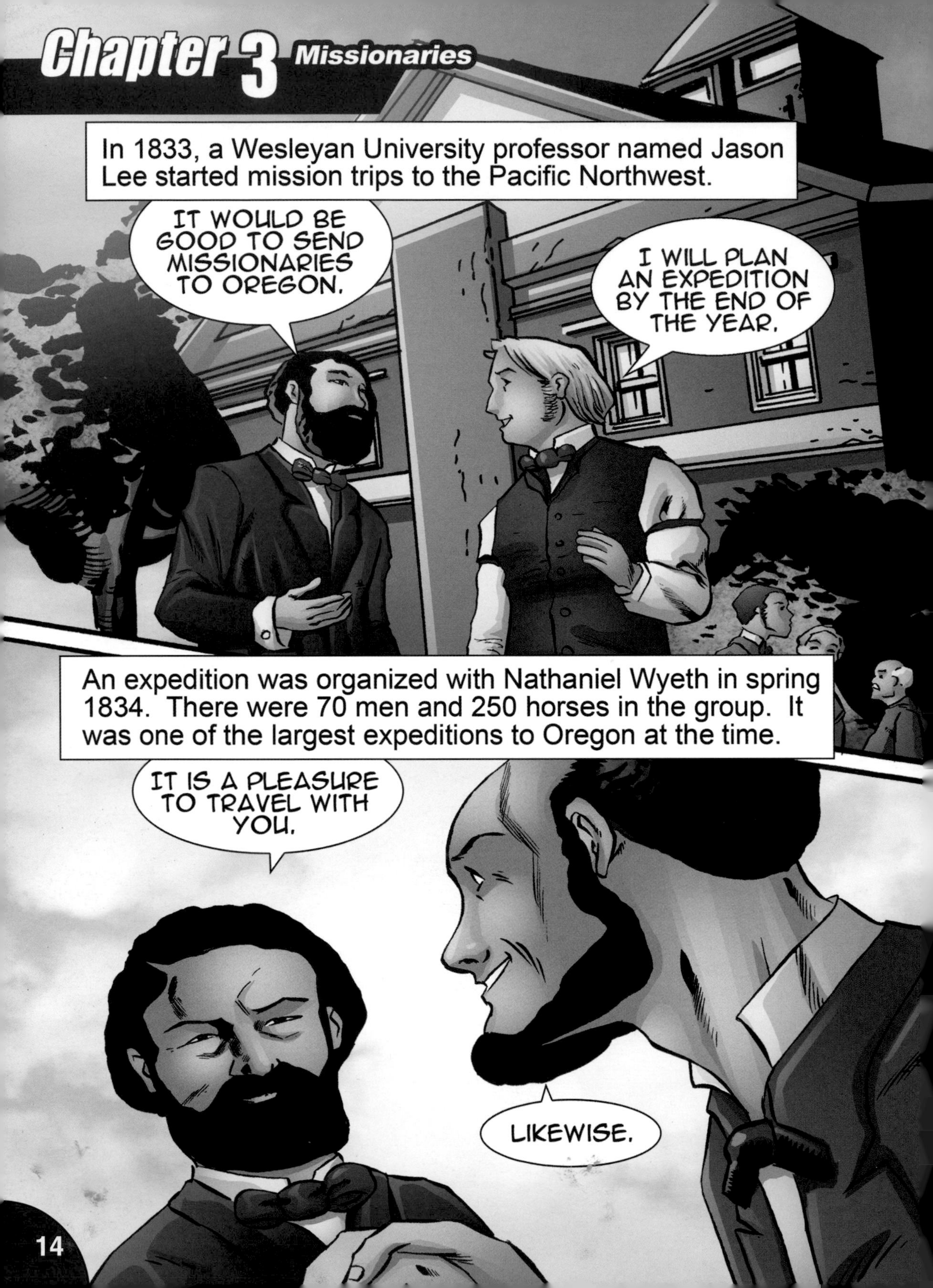
In 1833, a Wesleyan University professor named Jason Lee started mission trips to the Pacific Northwest.
IT WOULD BE GOOD TO SEND MISSIONARIES TO OREGON.
I WILL PLAN AN EXPEDITION BY THE END OF THE YEAR.
An expedition was organized with Nathaniel Wyeth in spring 1834. There were 70 men and 250 horses in the group. It was one of the largest expeditions to Oregon at the time.
IT IS A PLEASURE TO TRAVEL WITH YOU.
LIKEWISE.

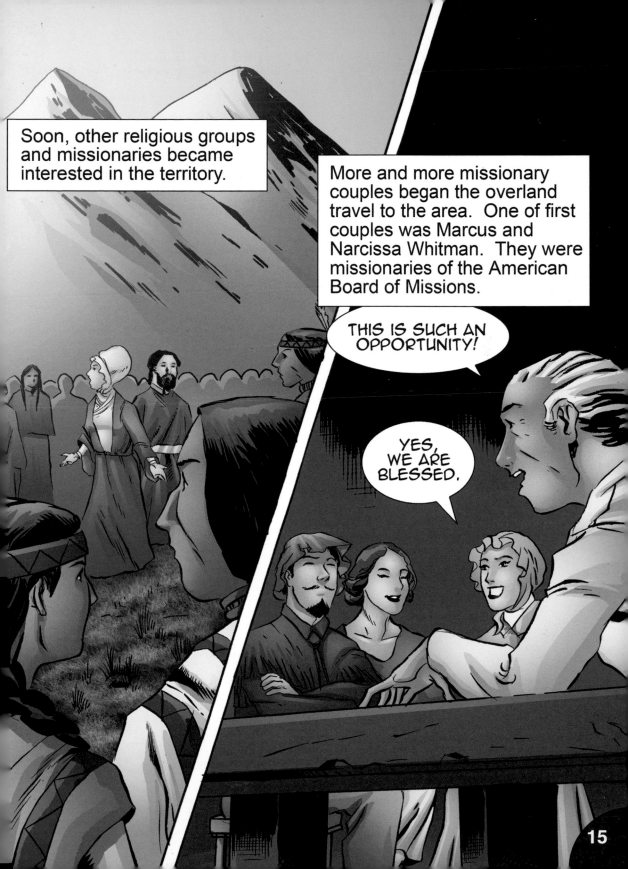

Soon, other religious groups and missionaries became interested in the territory.

More and more missionary couples began the overland travel to the area. One of first couples was Marcus and Narcissa Whitman. They were missionaries of the American Board of Missions.

THIS IS SUCH AN OPPORTUNITY!

YES, WE ARE BLESSED.

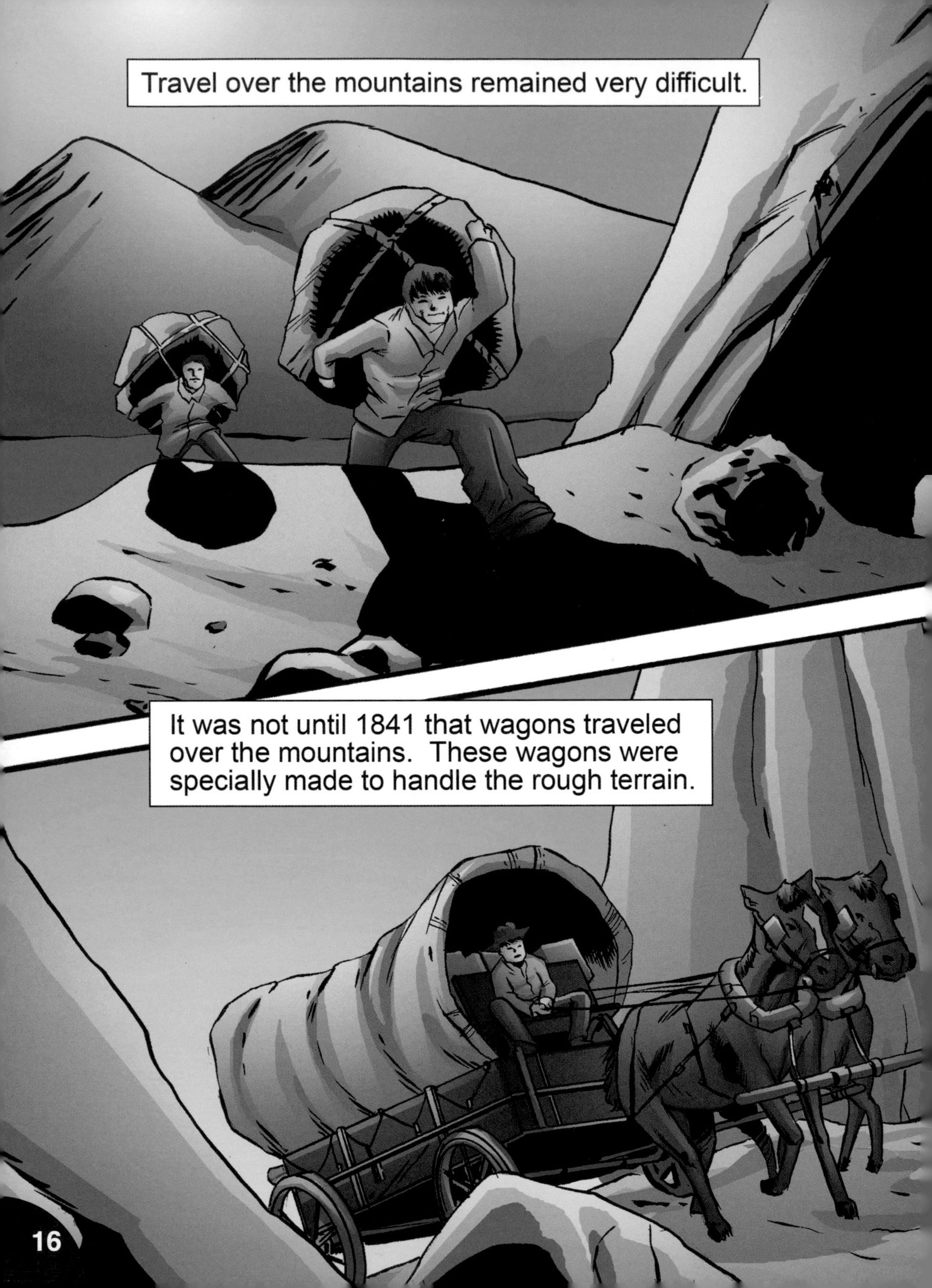
Travel over the mountains remained very difficult.
It was not until 1841 that wagons traveled over the mountains. These wagons were specially made to handle the rough terrain.

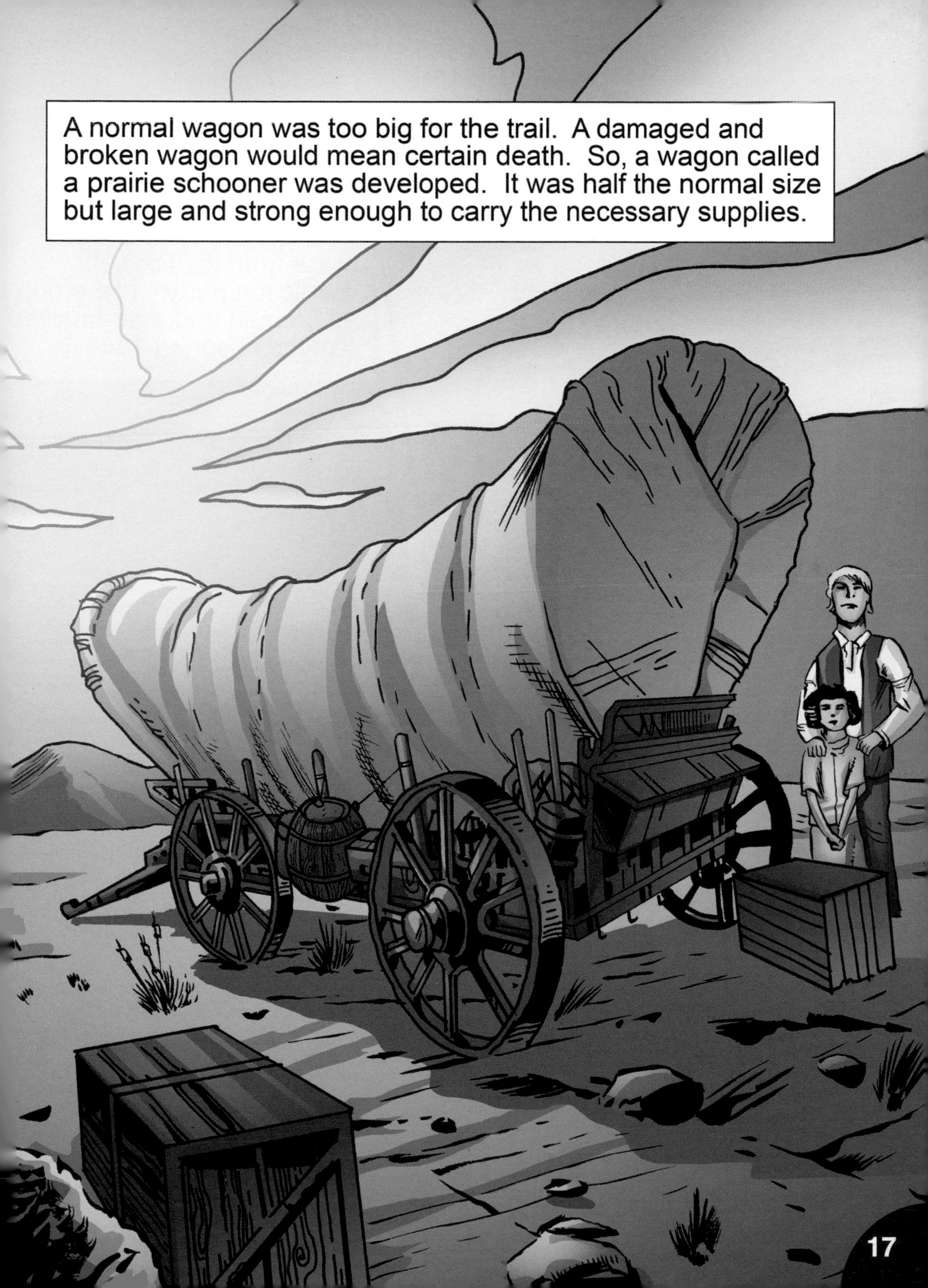
A normal wagon was too big for the trail. A damaged and broken wagon would mean certain death. So, a wagon called a prairie schooner was developed. It was half the normal size but large and strong enough to carry the necessary supplies.

Chapter 4 The First Emigrants

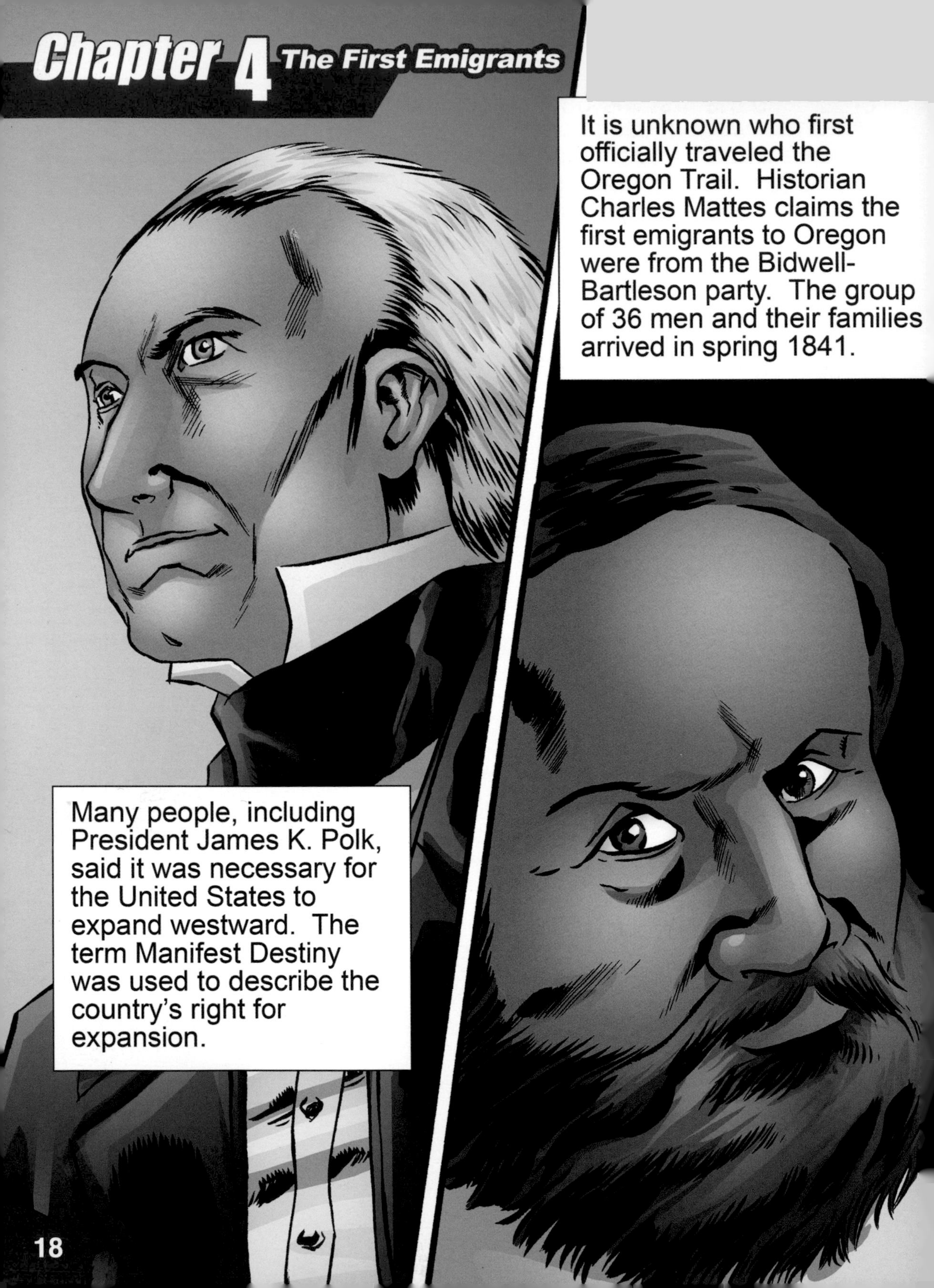
Many people, including President James K. Polk, said it was necessary for the United States to expand westward. The term Manifest Destiny was used to describe the country's right for expansion.
It is unknown who first officially traveled the Oregon Trail. Historian Charles Mattes claims the first emigrants to Oregon were from the Bidwell-Bartleson party. The group of 36 men and their families arrived in spring 1841.

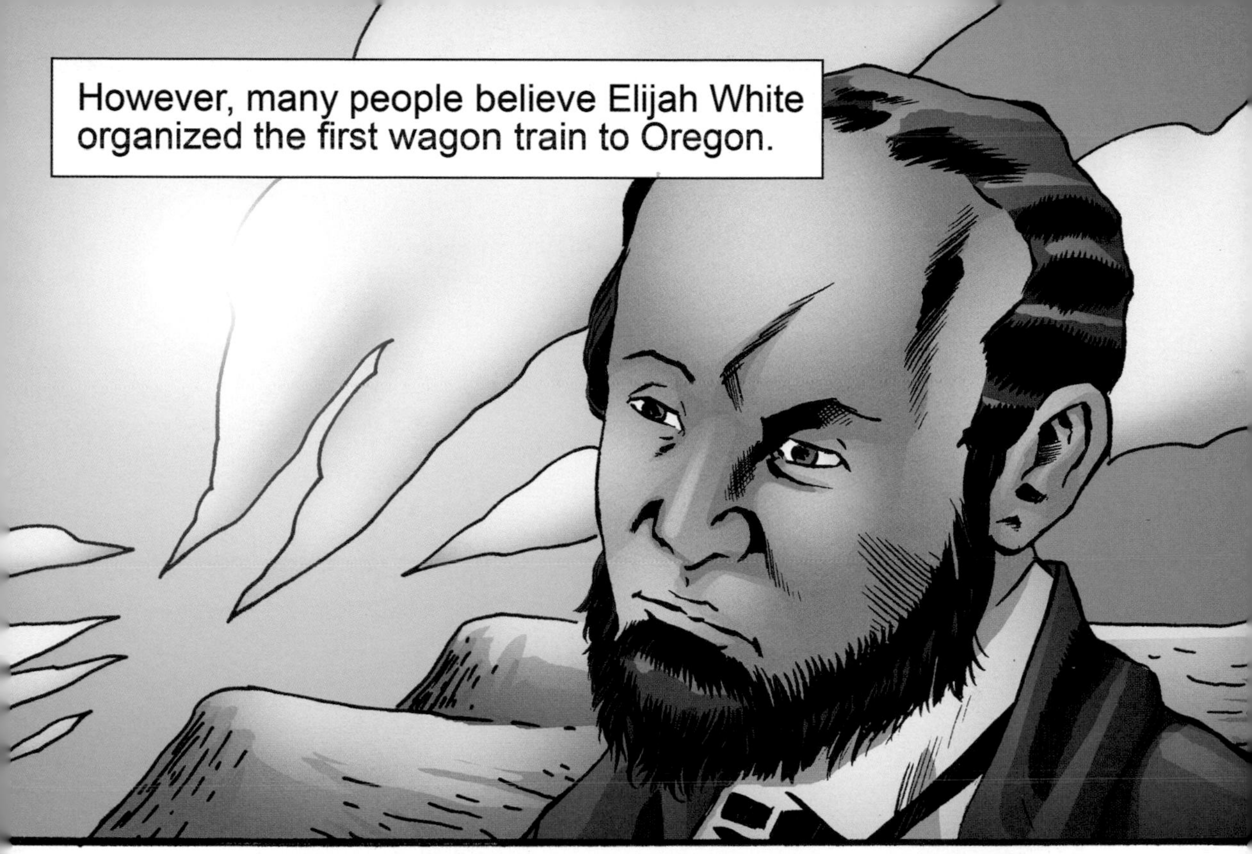
However, many people believe Elijah White organized the first wagon train to Oregon.

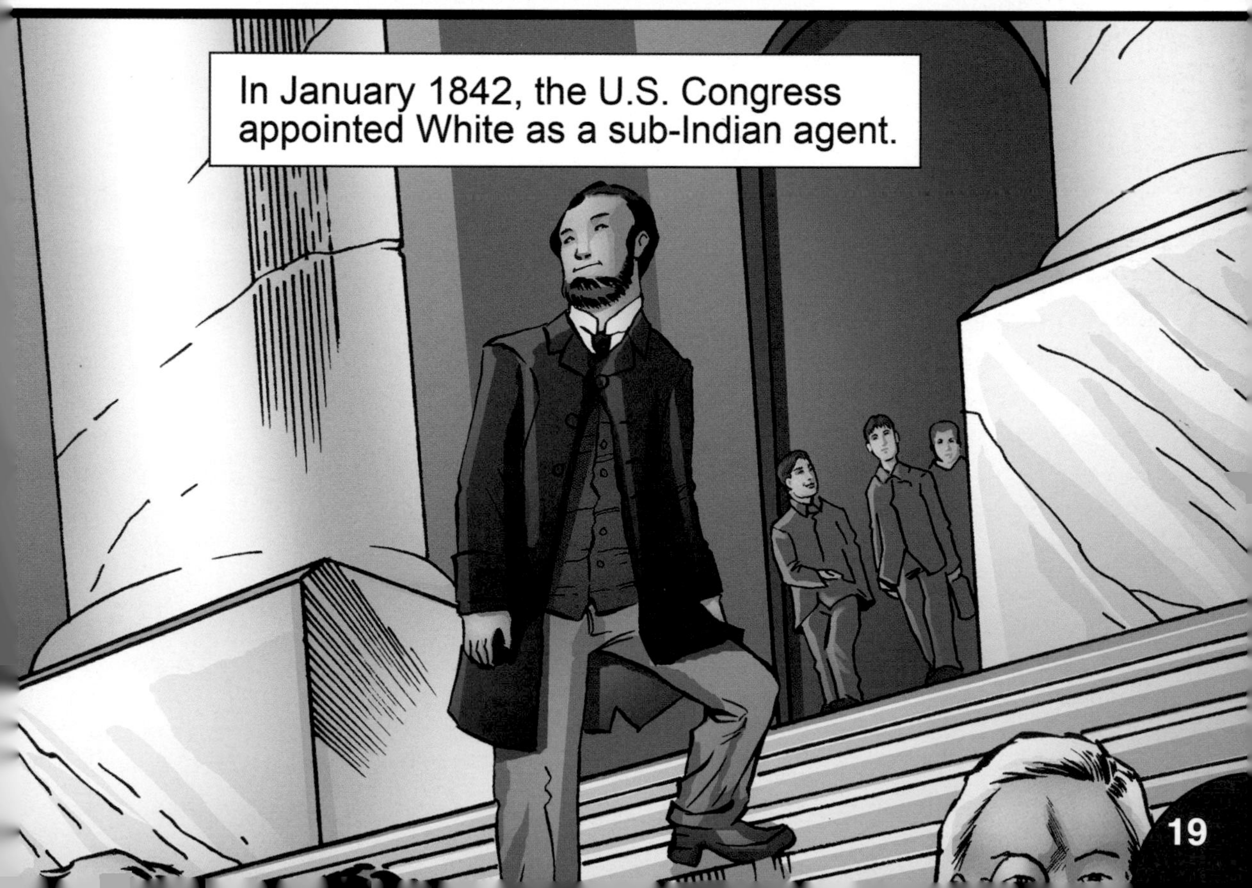
In January 1842, the U.S. Congress appointed White as a sub-Indian agent.

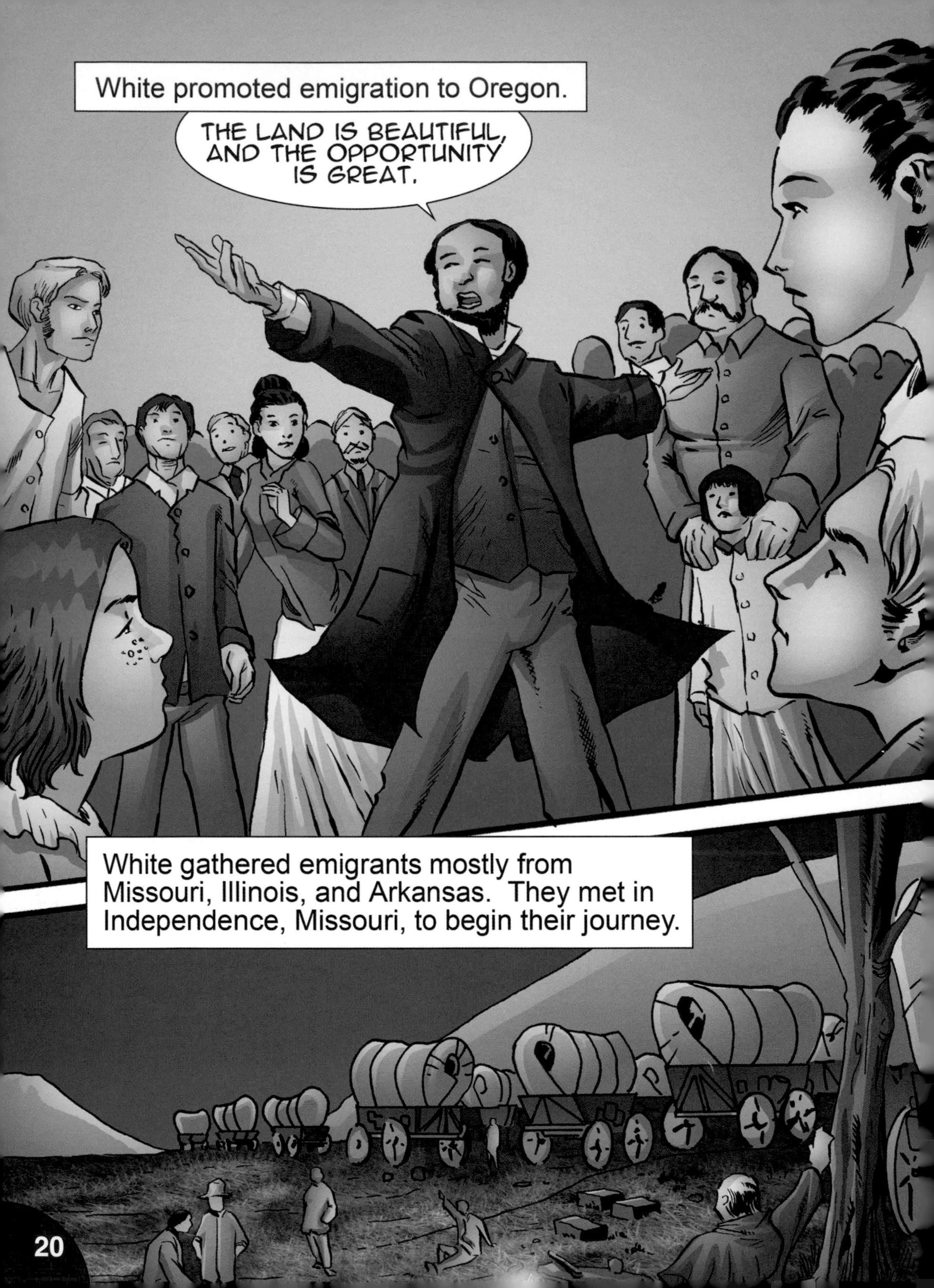
White promoted emigration to Oregon.
THE LAND IS BEAUTIFUL, AND THE OPPORTUNITY IS GREAT.
White gathered emigrants mostly from Missouri, Illinois, and Arkansas. They met in Independence, Missouri, to begin their journey.

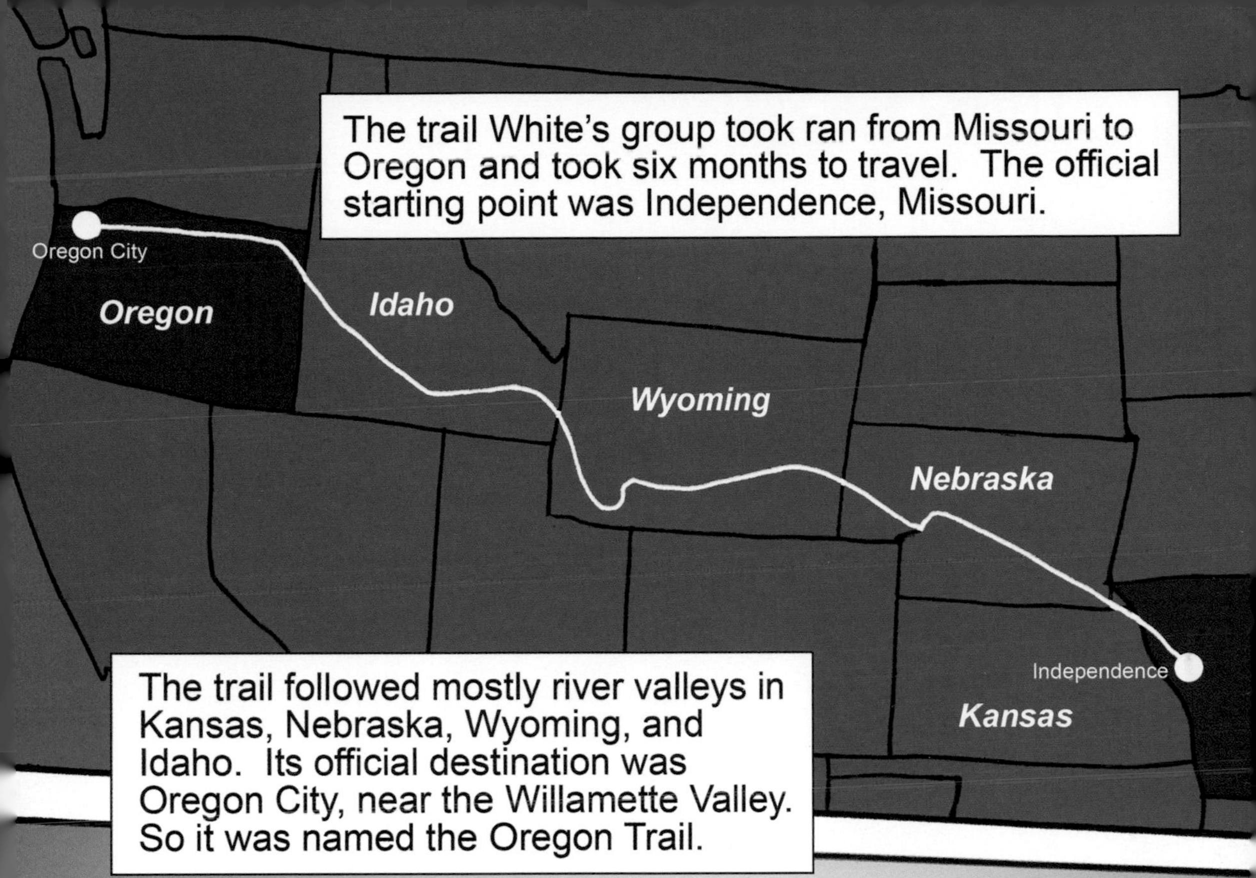
The trail White's group took ran from Missouri to Oregon and took six months to travel. The official starting point was Independence, Missouri.
Oregon City
Oregon
Idaho
Wyoming
Nebraska
Independence
Kansas
The trail followed mostly river valleys in Kansas, Nebraska, Wyoming, and Idaho. Its official destination was Oregon City, near the Willamette Valley. So it was named the Oregon Trail.

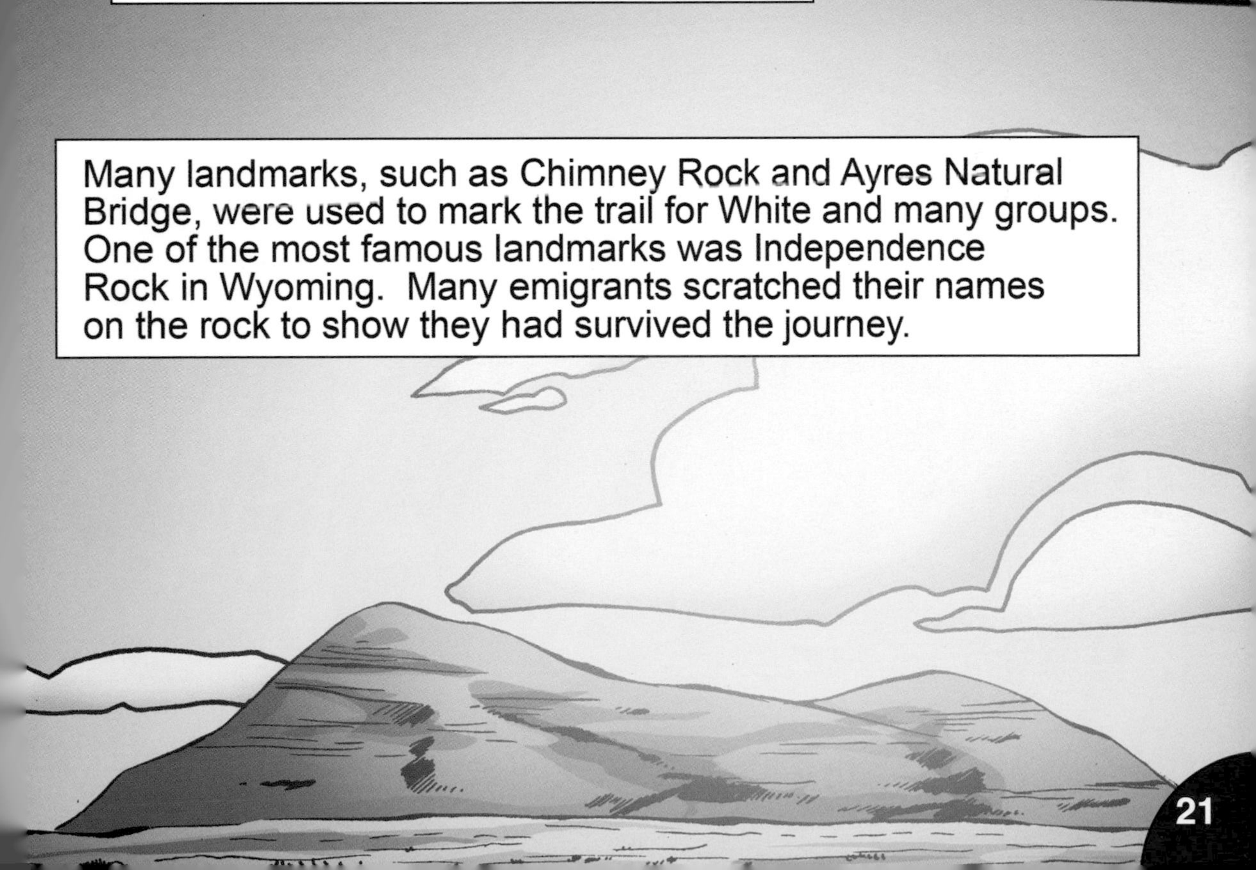
Many landmarks, such as Chimney Rock and Ayres Natural Bridge, were used to mark the trail for White and many groups. One of the most famous landmarks was Independence Rock in Wyoming. Many emigrants scratched their names on the rock to show they had survived the journey.

Chapter 5 Oregon Fever

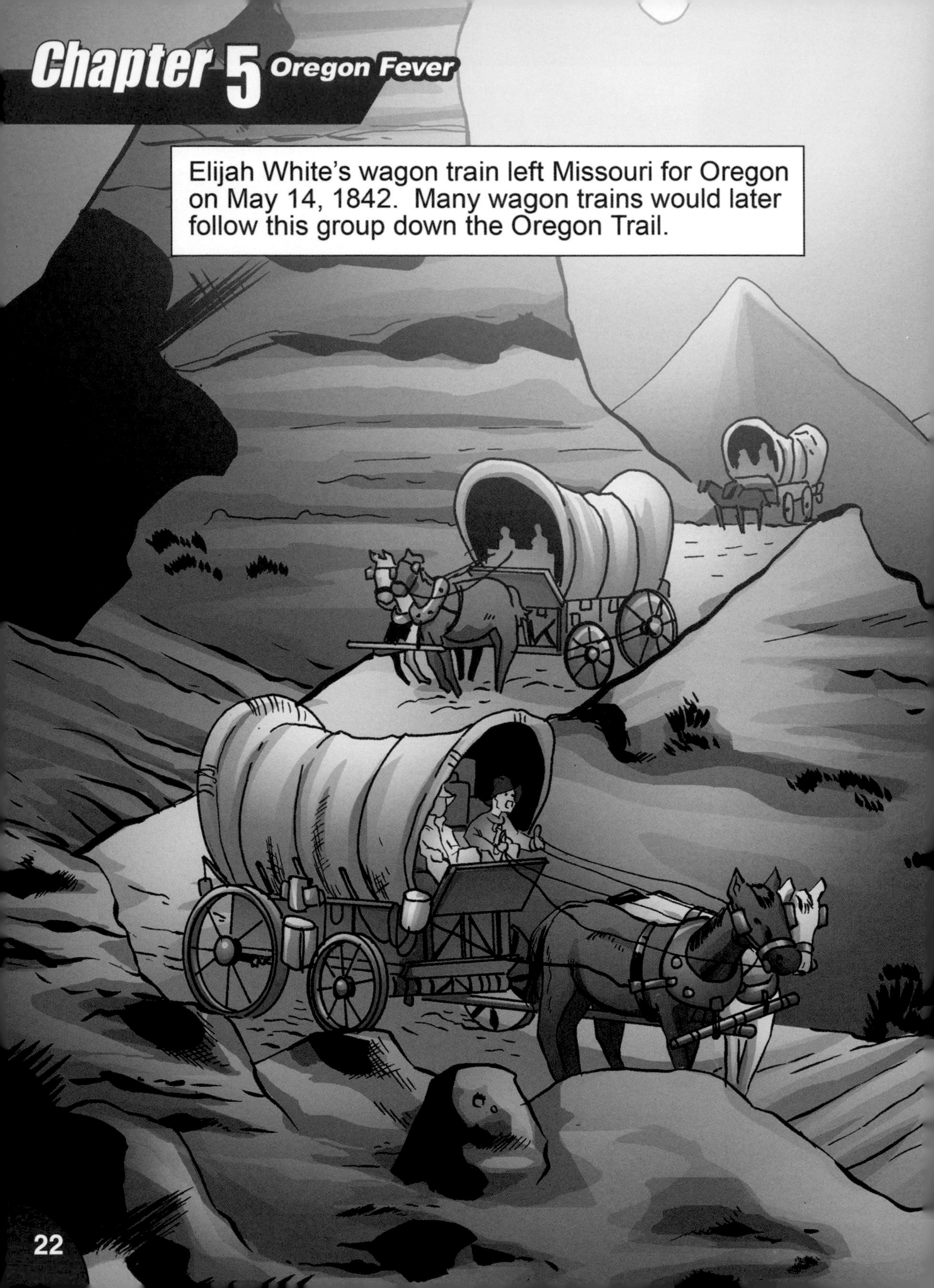
Elijah White's wagon train left Missouri for Oregon on May 14, 1842. Many wagon trains would later follow this group down the Oregon Trail.

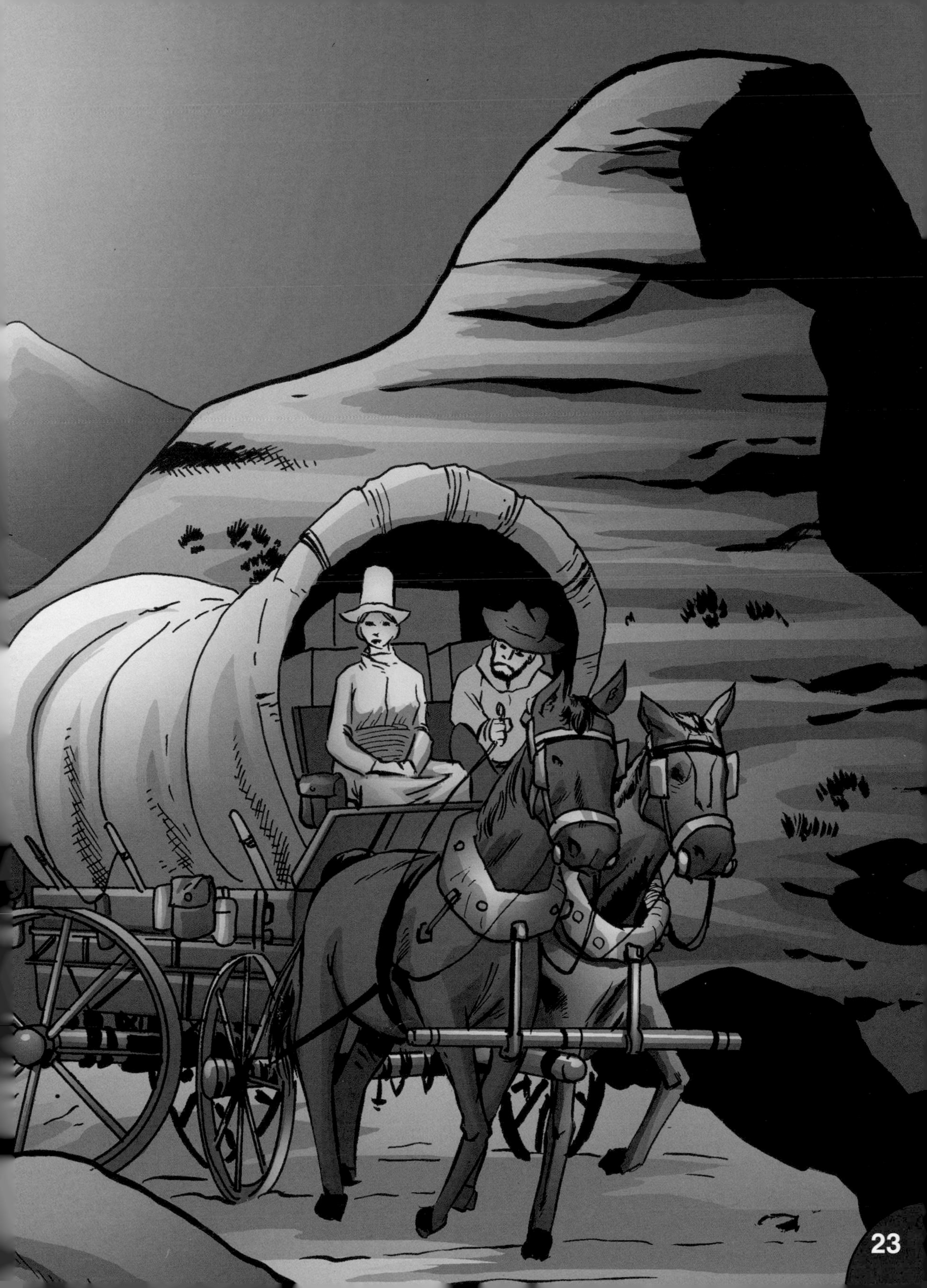

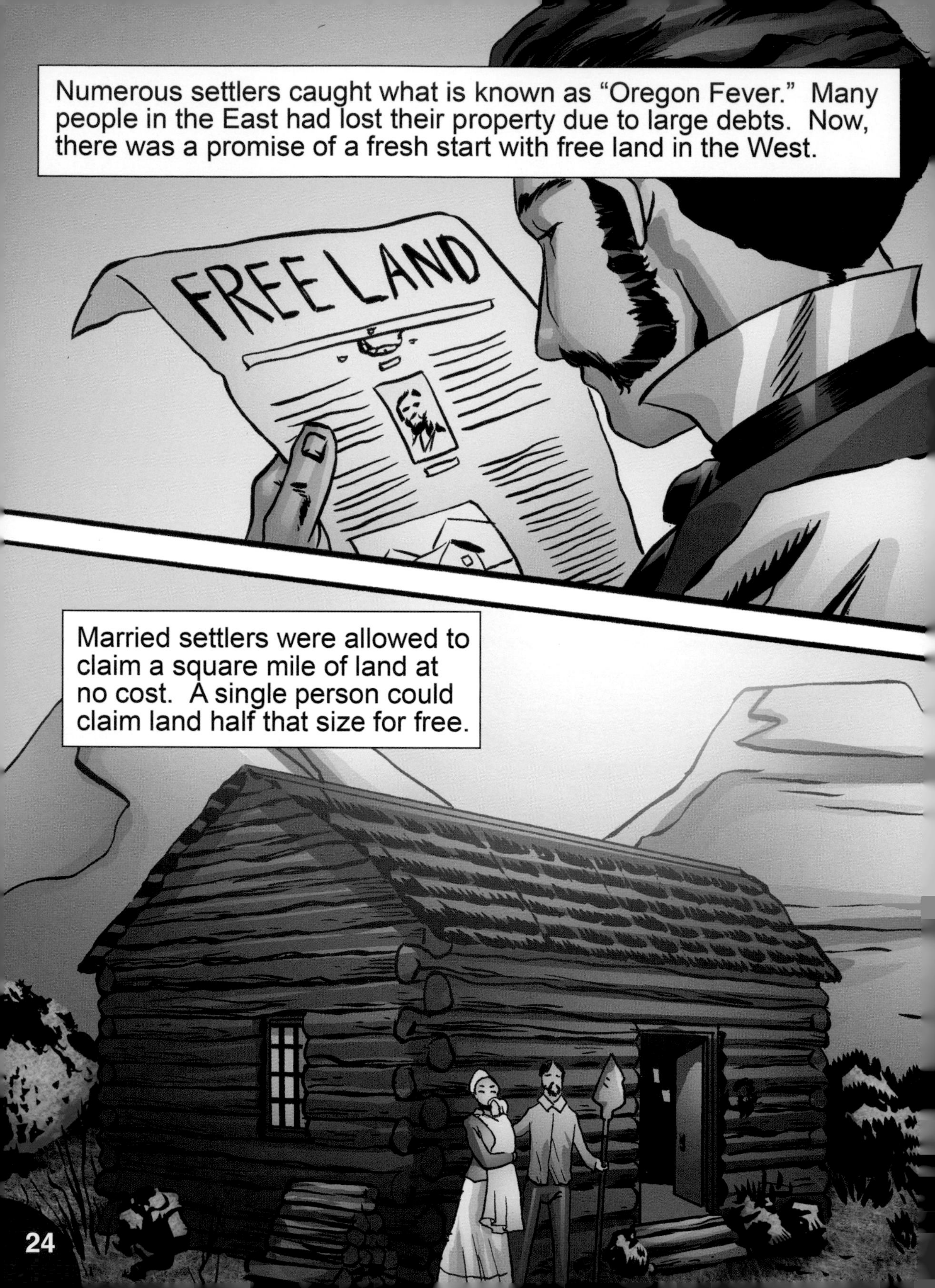
Numerous settlers caught what is known as “Oregon Fever.” Many people in the East had lost their property due to large debts. Now, there was a promise of a fresh start with free land in the West.
FREE LAND
Married settlers were allowed to claim a square mile of land at no cost. A single person could claim land half that size for free.

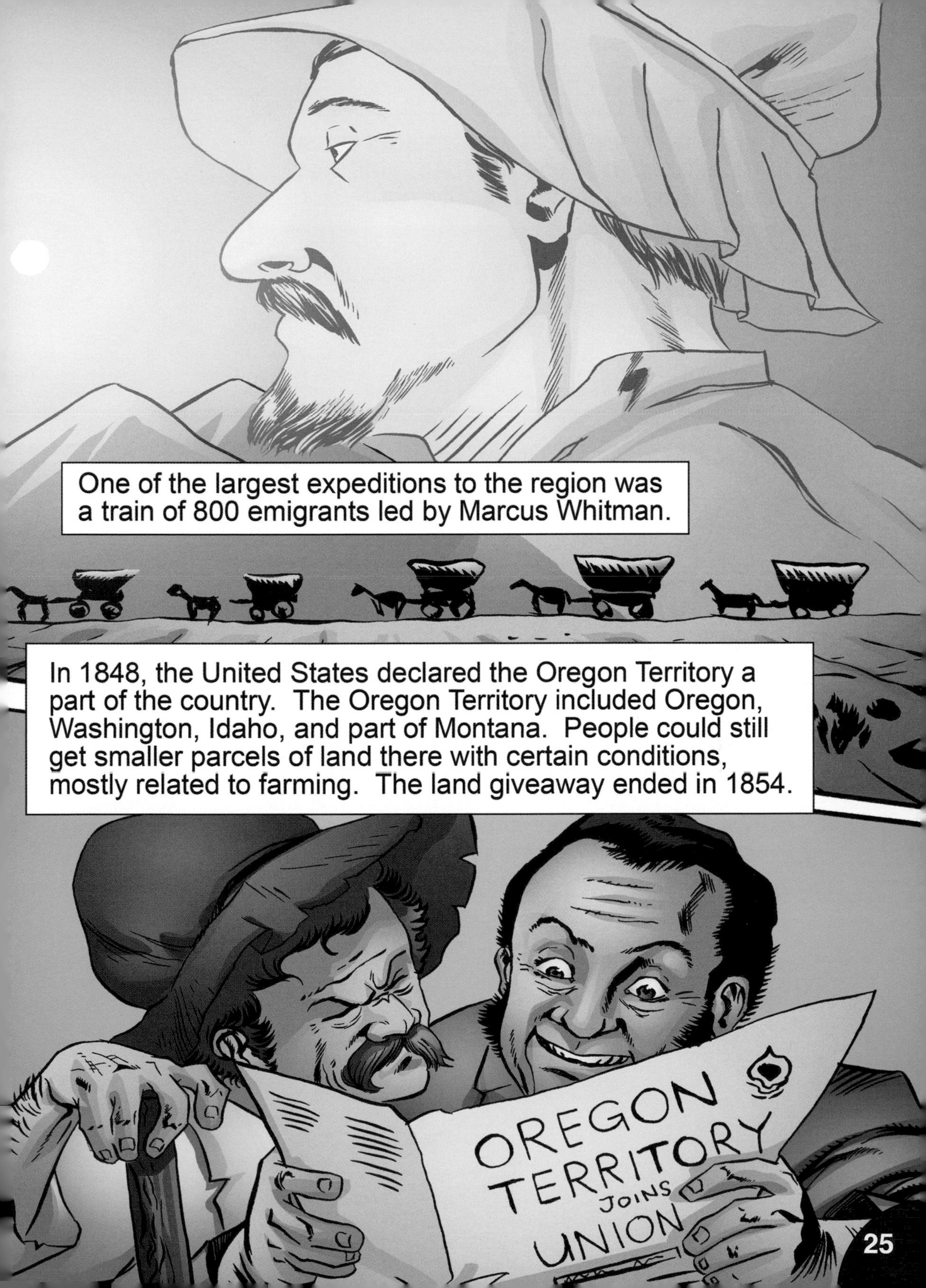
One of the largest expeditions to the region was a train of 800 emigrants led by Marcus Whitman.
In 1848, the United States declared the Oregon Territory a part of the country. The Oregon Territory included Oregon, Washington, Idaho, and part of Montana. People could still get smaller parcels of land there with certain conditions, mostly related to farming. The land giveaway ended in 1854.
OREGON TERRITORY JOINS UNION

Chapter 6 Enduring Legacy

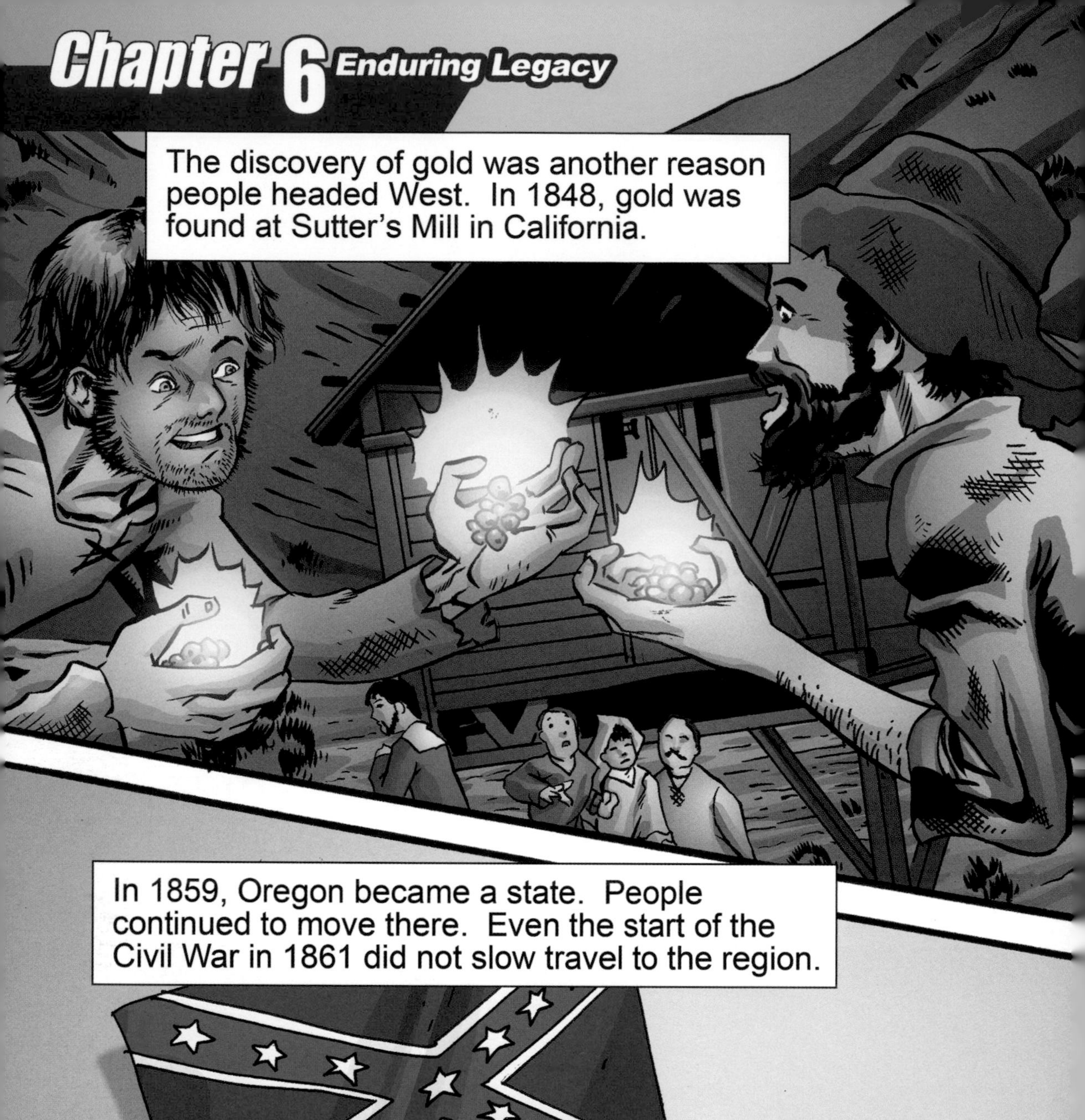
The discovery of gold was another reason people headed West. In 1848, gold was found at Sutter's Mill in California.

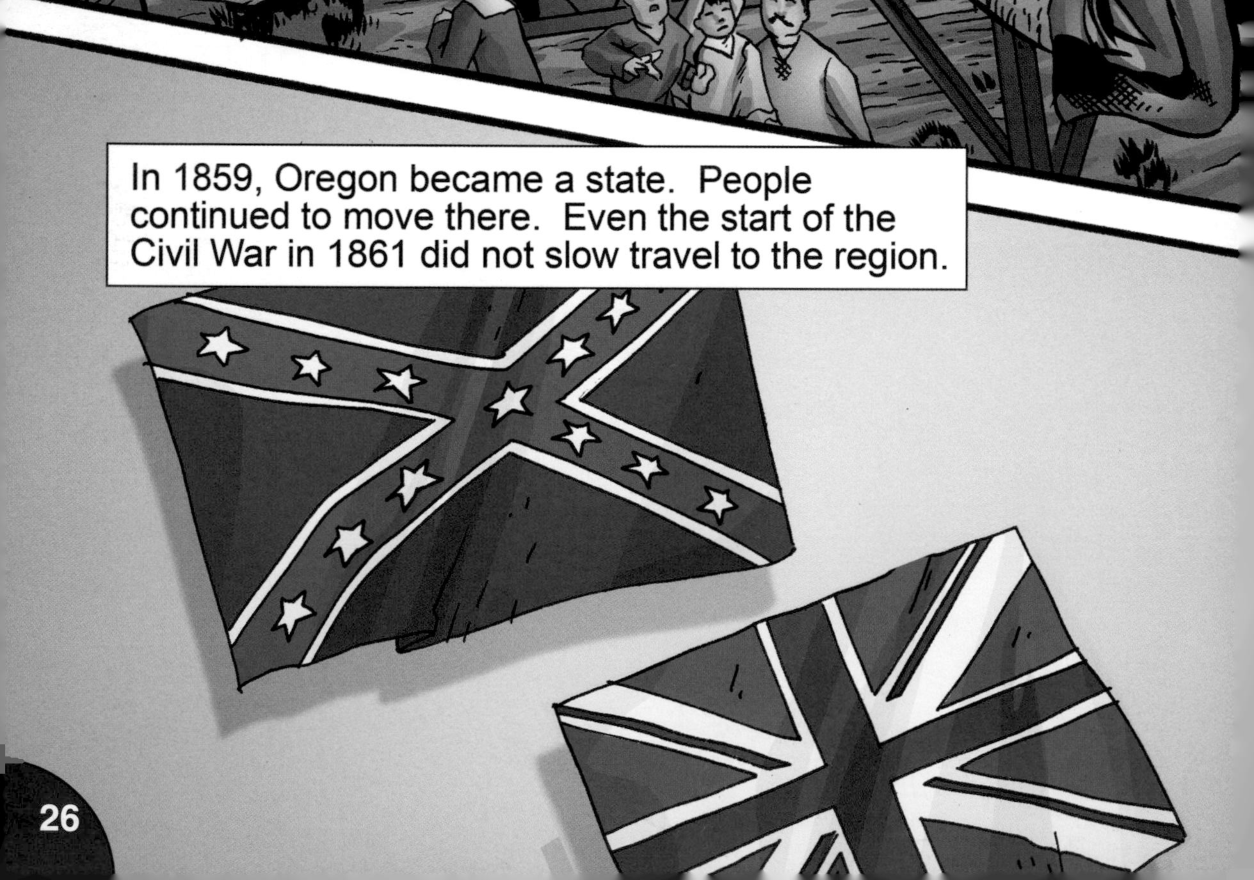
In 1859, Oregon became a state. People continued to move there. Even the start of the Civil War in 1861 did not slow travel to the region.

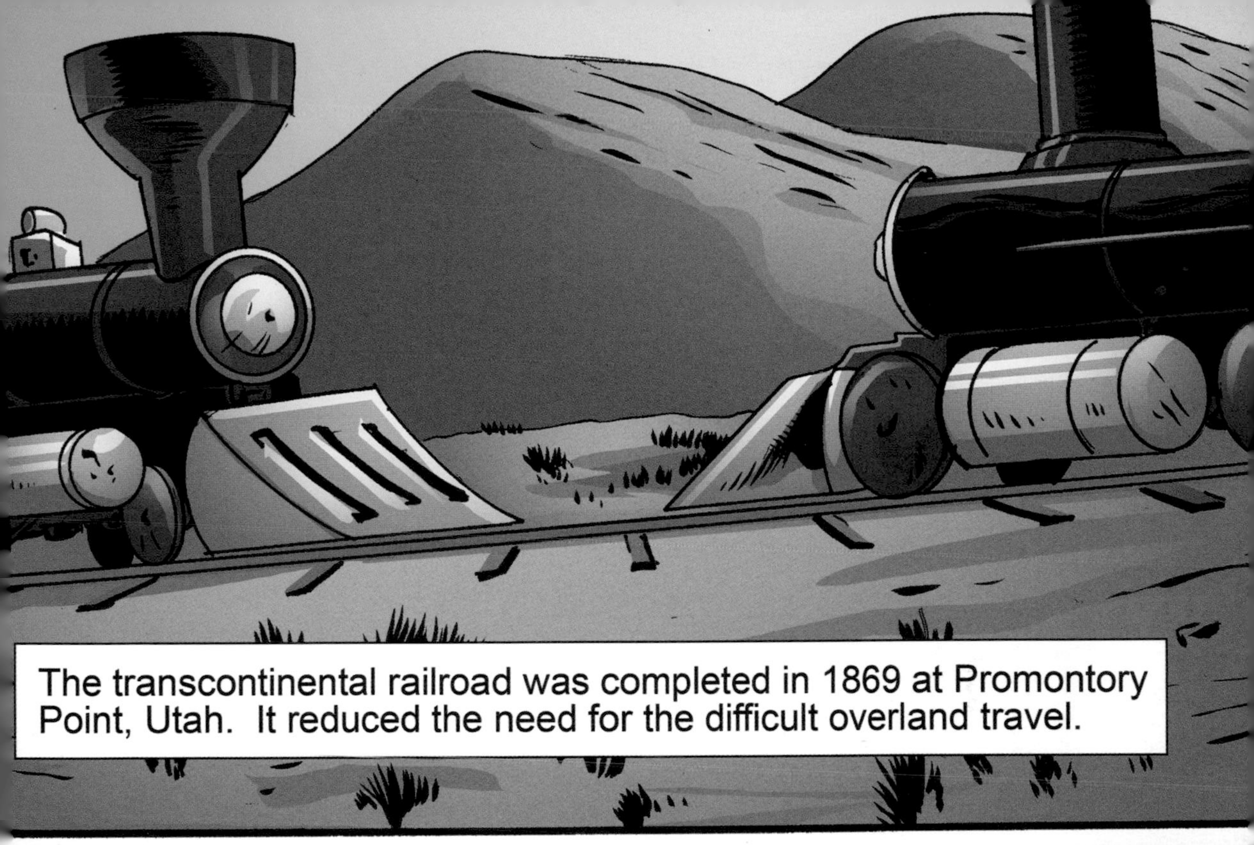
The transcontinental railroad was completed in 1869 at Promontory Point, Utah. It reduced the need for the difficult overland travel.

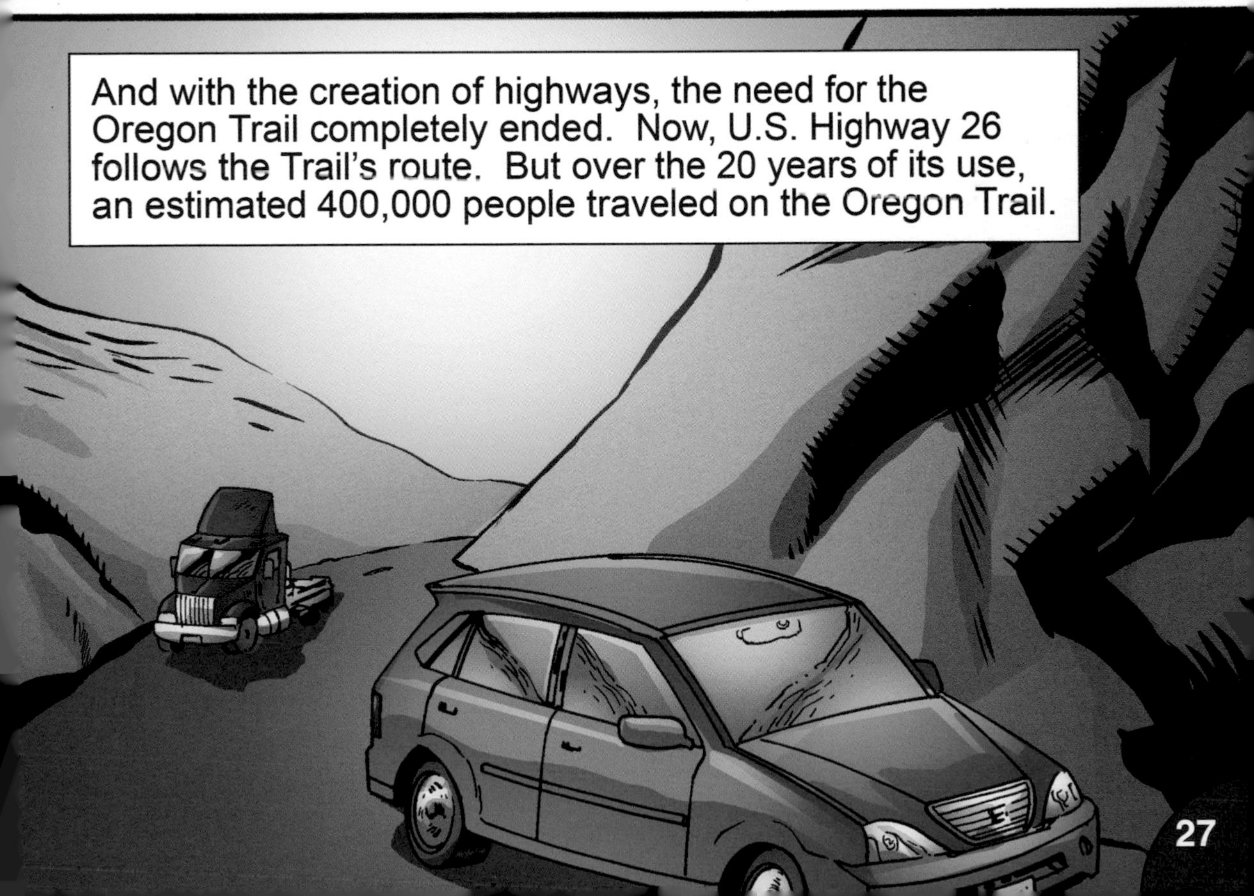
And with the creation of highways, the need for the Oregon Trail completely ended. Now, U.S. Highway 26 follows the Trail's route. But over the 20 years of its use, an estimated 400,000 people traveled on the Oregon Trail.

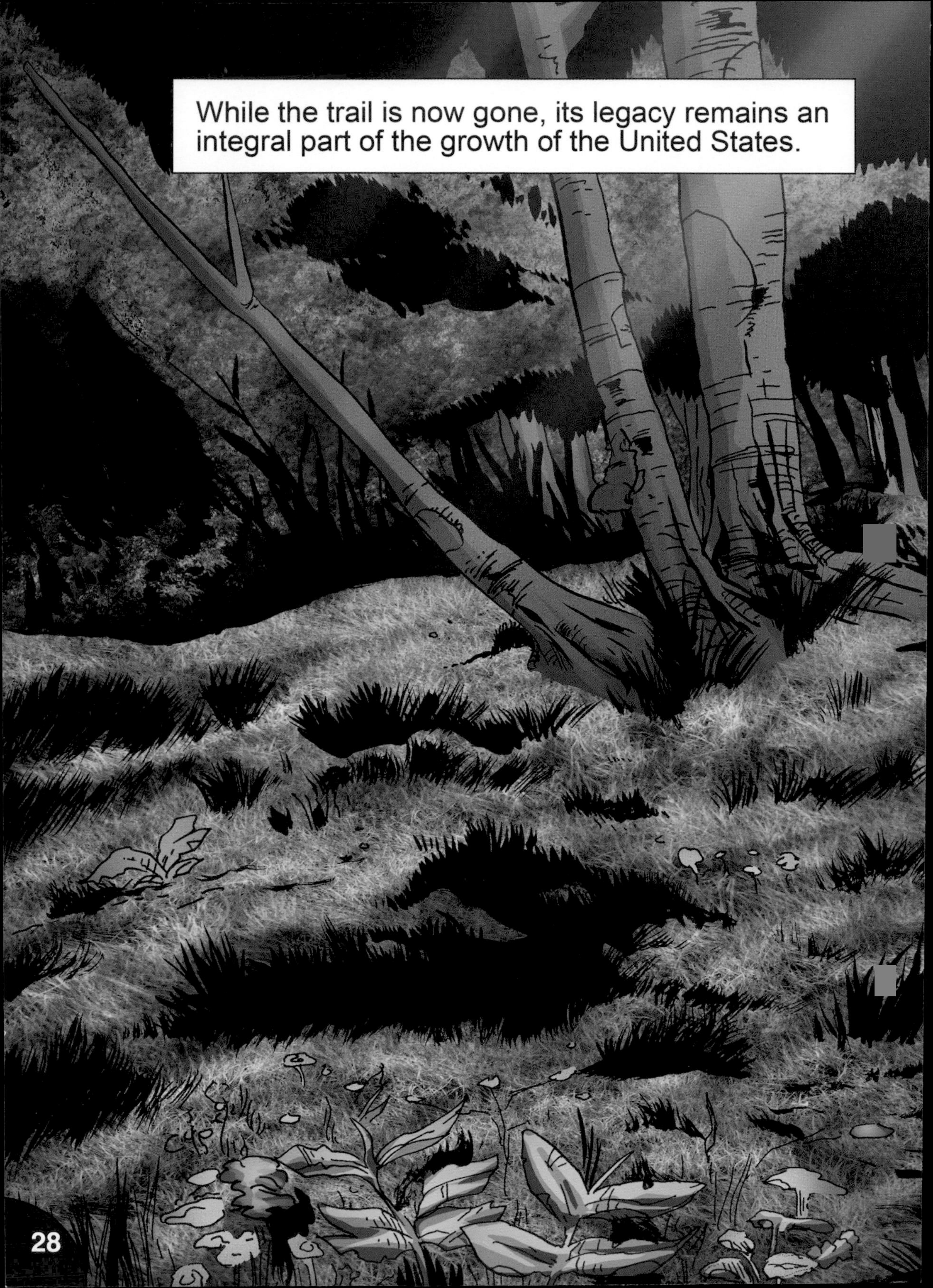
While the trail is now gone, its legacy remains an integral part of the growth of the United States.

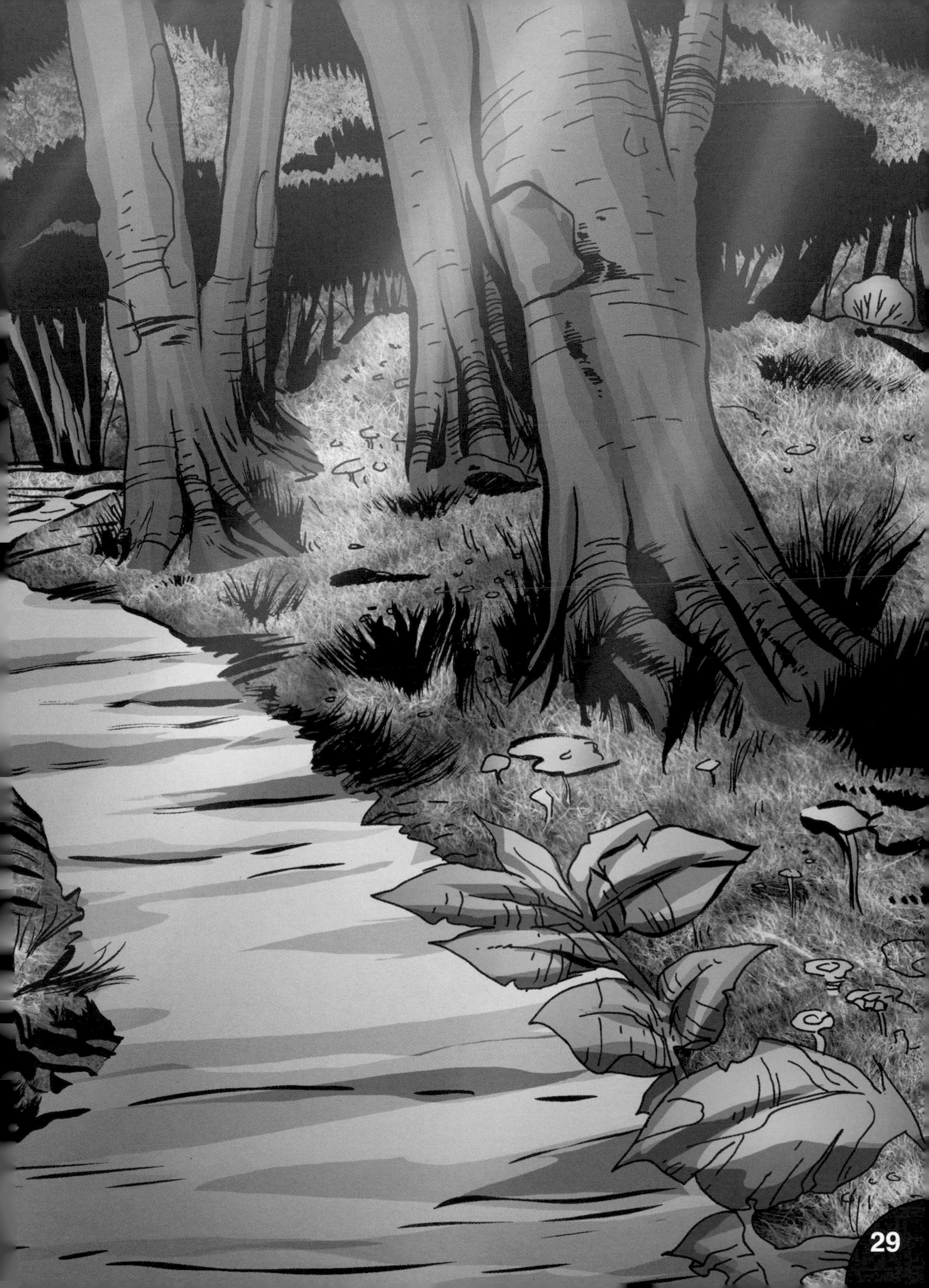

Fast Facts

• The move West was called "The Great Migration." Between 1843 and 1869, nearly half a million people moved West on the Oregon Trail.

• Washington, Oregon, California, Nevada, Idaho, and Utah would not be part of the United States today if not for the Oregon Trail.

• Marcus and Narcissa Whitman and Henry and Eliza Spalding were the first families to travel to Oregon. Today, a monument in Wyoming honors Narcissa and Eliza as the first women to travel across the Rocky Mountains.

• Though attacks by Native Americans were feared, and did occur, most contact was friendly. Natives helped travelers pull out stuck wagons and round up cattle. They also traded with the emigrants for horses and food.

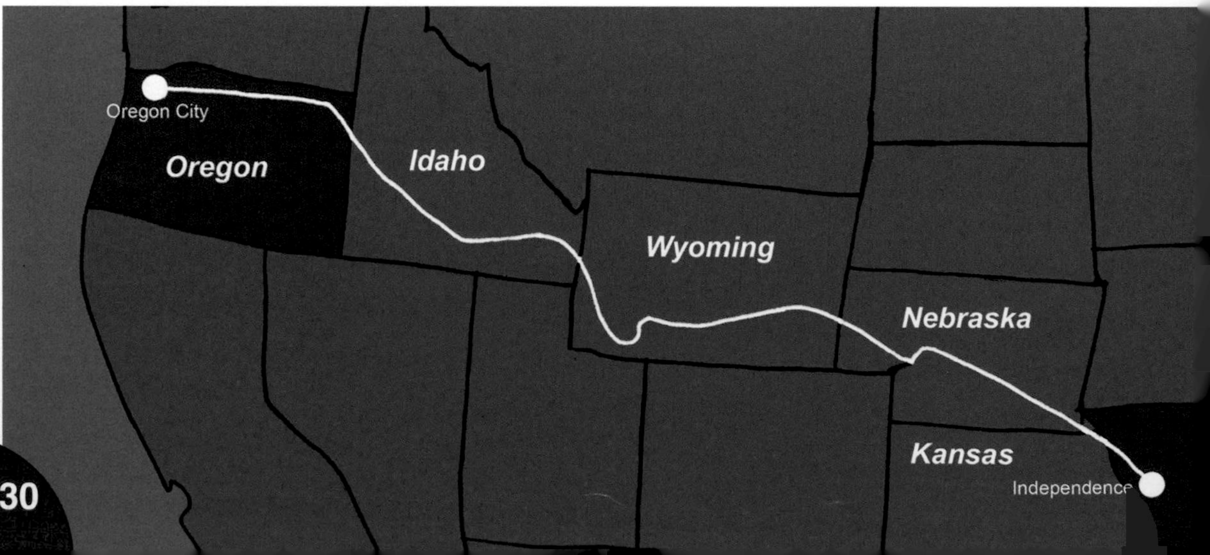
Oregon City
Oregon
Idaho
Wyoming
Nebraska
Kansas
Independence

Glossary

caravan - a group of people traveling together for safety through difficult or dangerous country.

civil war - a war between groups in the same country. The United States of America and the Confederate States of America fought a civil war from 1861 to 1865.

emigrate - to leave one area of a country and move to another. People who emigrate are called emigrants.

inhabit - to live in or occupy a region. A place where nothing lives is uninhabited.

integral - essential for completing an idea, task, or thought.

legacy - something left by a person or a group in the past.

missionary - a person who spreads a church's religion.

terrain - the physical features of an area of land. Mountains, rivers, and canyons can all be part of a terrain.

Web Sites

To learn more about the Oregon Trail, visit ABDO Publishing Company on the World Wide Web at **www.abdopublishing.com**. Web sites about the Oregon Trail are featured on our Book Links page. These links are routinely monitored and updated to provide the most current information available.

Index